LOVE.
MIL
& PAPER
CUTS

Susan Klingman

Running Press
Philadelphia, Pennsylvania

Canadian representatives: General Publishing Co., Ltd., 30 Lesmill Road, Don Mills, Ontario M3B 2T6.
International representatives: Worldwide Media Services, Inc., 115 East Twenty-third Street, New York, New York 10010.

9 8 7 6 5 4 3 2 1

Digit on the right indicates the number of this printing.
Library of Congress Cataloging-in-publication Number 91–52874
ISBN 1–56138–034–2
Cover design by Toby Schmidt
Interior design by Stephanie Longo
Illustration research by Gillian Speeth
Typography: ITC Cheltenham by Commcor Communications Corporation, Philadelphia, Pennsylvania
Printed in the United States

The woodcuts in this book were taken from *The Illustration of Books* by David Bland; *An Introduction to the History of Woodcut* Arthur M. Hind; *Graphic Worlds of Peter Bruegel the Elder*, edited by H. Arthur Klein; *An Introduction to the Woodcut of the Seventeenth Century* by Hellmut Lehmann–Haupt; and the following titles from the Dover Pictorial Archive Series: *Old English Cuts and Illustrations for Artists and Craftspeople*, edited by Bowles and Carver; *1800 Woodcuts by Thomas Bewick and His School*, edited by Blanche Carver; *Beasts and Animals*, edited by Konrad Gesner; *Picture Sourcebook for Collage and Decoupage*, edited by Edmund V. Gillon, Jr.; *3,800 Early Advertising Cuts*, edited by Carol Belanger Grafton; and *Symbols, Signs, and Signets*, edited by Ernst Lehner. Additional images were provided by the Free Library of Philadelphia, Print and Picture Department.

This book may be ordered by mail from the publisher. Please add $2.50 for postage and handling.
But try your bookstore first!
Running Press Book Publishers
125 South Twenty-second Street
Philadelphia, Pennsylvania 19103

DEDICATION

To my family, friends, co-workers, acquaintances, and political leaders, all of whom have added so much to my misery.

ACKNOWLEDGMENTS

A vast number of people contributed to this collection, directly and indirectly. To each of them I offer thanks. I am grateful to Lori Klingman, Joshua Klingman, Joan Hayes, Scott Looper, the person with the purple hippopotamus, Jon Winokur, and Greg Aaron and the staff at Running Press for their support and assistance. I am especially grateful to Dave Barry, whose work is a source of inspiration and whose kindness is a source of support; and Carey Luckman, counselor, confidant, and the only person I know who is as miserable as I am.

INTRODUCTION

Beyond my deep devotion to personal misery, I see a value in this work that is best illustrated by a story about King Solomon. It is a very old story from Jewish lore that has been handed down through the generations.

 King Solomon (so the story goes) was a thoughtful and caring leader. But he found himself deeply troubled by a problem even his great wisdom could not solve. Whenever King Solomon was very sad, he felt as though he had always been sad, and that he would

5

always be sad. This, of course, was extremely uncomfortable for the king. Equally troublesome to him was that whenever he was very happy, he felt as though he had always been happy and would always be happy. The king worried that he would become caught in these extremes and forget the problems of his people.

In an attempt to find a solution, King Solomon sent out a call across the land, asking for his subjects' help. They came from far and wide, bringing jewels, mystical cures, medicines, and all sorts of advice. The king saw them one by one, but none could cure his woe.

The audiences continued for many days without success, and finally only one subject remained in the line. He was an old beggar, dressed in rags and carrying a tattered cloth bag.

The king's advisors scoffed. "What can this beggar man possibly offer that the richest, smartest, most powerful people in the kingdom could not?" they asked. But the king insisted on seeing the beggar.

He came humbly to King Solomon's feet, knelt, and drew from his bag a tarnished, dented silver ring. He offered the ring to the king and said, "This will solve your problem, Your Highness."

King Solomon examined the ring, but he could not fathom the old beggar's meaning. "I do not understand," said the king. "How will this help me?"

"Read the inscription on the ring," the beggar replied.

"'*Gem Zeh Ya'avor*,'" read the king. "'This Too Shall Pass.'"

The beggar said, "Whenever you are very sad, just look at this ring and you will be reminded that 'This Too Shall Pass.' And whenever you are very happy, look at the ring, and you will also be reminded that, 'This Too Shall Pass.'"

And so the beggar left, carrying a bag of gold coins that the king gave him in appreciation. King Solomon put on the ring and never took it off. Whenever he was very

happy, and whenever he was very sad, he looked to the ring.

I hope that in some small way this book can be your "King Solomon's ring." When you're unhappy or frustrated, perhaps this book will offer you comfort and laughs. And when you are happy, perhaps you will want to remind yourself that ours is a world fraught with troubles. Either way you choose to look at it, "This Too Shall Pass."

Life's but a walking shadow, a poor player,
That struts and frets his hour upon the stage,
And then is heard no more. It is a tale
Told by an idiot, full of sound and fury,
Signifying nothing.

—William Shakespeare
Macbeth, Act V, scene v

"The fact that if Elvis were alive today he'd probably be dead by now."—Dave Barry

fractals

missing your dog

great green gobs of gory, gushy gorilla guts with monkey vomit sauce

$E=MC^2$

this business of living

Type A personalities

"A thousand points of light"

child abandonment

abduction

aberrations

abnormality

the Abominable Snowman

aborting a mission

abortion

people who believe they are above the law

abridged editions

an indefinite leave of absence

"absence makes the heart grow fonder"

The absent-minded

being marked absent when you are present

absentee parents

absurdity

staring directly into the abyss

academic probation

academese

forgetting your access code

accidentally overhearing people having sex

people who stop and stare at accidents

being accident-prone

pretending that whatever it is you did
accidentally was actually what you had in
mind all along

not getting anything accomplished

accordion music

accountability

accountants

bad acoustics

losing your ace in the hole

aches, pains, fever, and chills

dubious achievements

your Achilles' heel

acid burns

acid indigestion

acid rain

anti-aircraft fire

acne

acronyms

people who don't act their age

putting on an act

acts of God

bad actors

being called up for active duty

realizing that you have ceased to be an activist

puff adders

being addicted to addiction

feeling addled

addresses and phone numbers flashed on the TV screen so fast you can't write them down

ad hoc committees

adjusting

administrative hearings

adulthood

EVEN WORSE: childhood

THE WORST: adolescence

adult themes

adversity

before and after pictures in diet ads that don't look like they show the same people

people in health club ads who don't look like they need health clubs

perfume ads

public service ads by oil companies

advertising calendars

aerobics

aerosol cans that won't spray

aerosol cheese

getting your affairs in order

affirmative action

Afghanistan

the aftermath of war

afterthoughts

age spots

Agent Orange

"Enquiring minds want to know"

aging rock stars

agitprop

agnosticism

the agony of defeat

aggravated assault

agreeing to do something that you actually have no intention of carrying out

agreeing to disagree

naked aggression

getting too far ahead of yourself

discovering someone you know is dying of AIDS

ailumania: the irrational desire for cats

people who insist "ain't" is a word

people who put on airs

not having air conditioning

the Air Force

recipes from the airline food service

nonrefundable airline tickets

airport security

airports the day before a holiday

cars that say "the door is ajar"

AK-47s

Akron, Ohio

forgetting to turn off the alarm on a day you don't have to get up

forgetting to set the alarm

missing the extra hour of sleep you could have had if you had remembered to set the clock back for Daylight Savings Time

an albatross around your neck

alcohol abuse among airline pilots

Horatio Alger stories

algebra

aliases

alienation

having to come up with an alibi

illegal aliens

alien life forms

Alcatraz

allegations

"Life is divided into the horrible and the
miserable."— Woody Allen

allergies

the amount of contaminants the F.D.A. allows
into the food it approves

the allowance you received as a child that
was never enough

shopkeepers who act as though they are
doing you a favor by *allowing* you the honor
of buying their goods

allusions

your alma mater

going it alone

when you have all of your record albums in
alphabetical order and someone messes them
up

when they break into the program you are
watching, and then return to it "already in
progress"

amateurs

the Amazon

ambiguities

ambulance chasers

ambulatory vegetables

being ambushed

slices of Americana

amnesia

"Amos and Andy"

knowing you have amounted to all you are ever going to

amputation

Amtrak

anabolic steroids

anachronisms

analgesic rubs

anomalies

anarchy

being charged full price for putting an ingredient on only half the pizza

andromania: the insane need for men

anesthesia that doesn't work

angry young men

looking at things from many angles

angst

anguish

animals chewing off their own legs to get out of traps

animals knocking over your garbage cans

attributing human personality traits to animals

swollen ankles

announcements

anorexia nervosa

needing an antidote

annulments

boring answering machine messages

people with all the answers

EVEN WORSE: not having any answers yourself

burning ants with a magnifying glass

feeling antsy

not developing proper antibodies

anticipating trouble

the anticlimax

anti-choice propagandists

people who continue to believe that antidisestablishmentarianism is the longest word in the English language

anti-heroes

antitank weapons

antiquated bridges

free-floating anxiety

anything

apartheid

Apocalypse Now

apologies from people you know don't mean it

apostasy

concern with appearances

an appendix to a supplement

appendicitis

an insatiable appetite

grainy apples

April Fool's Day

April 15th

apron strings

the Age of Aquarius

Arab-Israeli relations

arcade games

archaic words

ugly architecture

circular arguments

when your argument falls on deaf ears

aristocracy

the arms race

the United States selling arms to our enemies

armpit noises

the Army

new arrangements of old songs

being in arrears

being arrested

"[America] is the only country where failing to promote yourself is regarded as arrogant."—Garry Trudeau

arsenic

life imitating art

art imitating life

those who would define art

artful dodging

arthritis

that yucky, prickly stuff you have to clean off to get to artichoke hearts

when you are reading an article in a newspaper or magazine and they keep continuing it somewhere else, and then you can't find the end

artificial intelligence

playing on artificial turf

"starving artists' sales"

artistic temperament

people who ask you how you are but don't wait for the answer

people who ask you about something you just said

A.S.K.I.A.: The American Society of Know-it-alls

low aspirations

aspirating vomit while under general anesthesia

looking at things assbackwards

assassins

"some assembly required"

getting to class and realizing that you left your assignment at home

falling asleep at the wheel

mistaken assumptions

astrology

asylums

atheists who say "God bless you"

athlete's foot

when you're so hung over you can feel atoms banging into your head

mental atrophy

Attack of the Killer Tomatoes

lawmakers with poor attendance records

getting locked in the attic when no one is home

a poor attitude

Attila the Hun

attorney's fees

District Attorneys dating Public Defenders

inadvertently bidding on something at an auction

audits

smelly old aunts who pinch your cheeks and leave lipstick prints on your forehead

when your favorite author's long-awaited book is bad

automated teller machines

auto mechanics

autophobia: the irrational fear of one's self

multiple autopsies

autoeroticism

being caught in an avalanche

the avant-garde

avarice

being avoided

Avon ladies

awkward moments

waiting for the ax to fall

having an ax to grind

psychotic babblings

when babies are afraid of you

the fear that you'll somehow crush the soft spot of a baby's head

babies getting their heads stuck between the bars of cribs

trying to find a babysitter

when you have just given birth and your new baby looks horrible

babysitting for other people's sick children

people who take their babies to the movies, and don't leave when the babies begin screaming

when your baby leaves you

backaches

backseat drivers

backtracking

forgetting to make backup disks

artificial bacon

bacteria

"Oh, it's not that bad"

when you are made out to be the bad guy

bad habits

being in a perpetually bad mood

a bad reputation

the bad seed

having a bad taste in your mouth

bagpipes

baggage checks

when the bagpeople pack your groceries poorly and you end up with squished bread, pureed fruit, and a nice big package of cookie crumbs

bagworms

not being able to make bail

"bait and switch"

Jim and Tammy Faye Bakker

bald spots

the way the ball bounces

playing ball in the house and breaking something

the old ball and chain

society balls

ball park food

EVEN WORSE: the cost of ball park food

portly ballerinas

ballroom dancing

being had by the balls

when Bambi's mother is killed

bamboo shoots under your fingernails

bananas that turn brown in a day

grabbing the banister and having it pull right off the wall

bank heists

trying to get money out of a piggy bank without breaking it

being turned down for a loan

when your banker jumps out of the window

when the people who owe you *lots* of money declare bankruptcy

barcodes

barflys

bars on your windows

barbarians

barbecues that won't start

Barbie and Ken

Robert Redford's drunken spree in *Barefoot in the Park*

really great bargains on things you don't need

barophobia: the abnormal fear of gravity

baroque religious art

barracudas

barrettes that scrape your scalp

barricades

two strikes, the bottom of the ninth, trailing by one point, a park full of bloodthirsty fans, and *you're* the batter

baseball players who move their cups around only while they are on camera

the American League

the National League

deflated basketballs

basement seepage

Norman Bates

bats in your belfry

needing a bath

how you look in a bathing suit

having to put wet bathing suits in your luggage

public bathrooms with no doors on the stalls

camping in the rain and having to go to the bathroom in the middle of the night

going to the bathroom when other people can hear

regrouting the bathtub

reading in the tub and dropping your book

coed dorm bathrooms

baton twirlers

dead batteries

the battery on your watch running out

battle plans

the battle of the sexes

the Bay of Pigs

foot-long bayonets

all the things you will never be

having to be in two places at one time

beaches closed due to pollution

trying to beat the system

debating who was the best Beatle

beauty contests

Beelzebub

beverages in plastic bottles

Bhopal

biases

the Bible Belt

trying to find a source someone has listed in their bibliography and discovering it doesn't exist

bicyclists riding three or four abreast

big business

Big Brother

big mouths

bigotry

falling out of your bikini top

string bikinis

Bildungsromans

bilge water

billboards

computer-generated bills for $0.00 that they insist on continuing to send you, no matter what you do to get them to stop

when all the bills from the holidays start coming in

the erosion of the Bill of Rights

billy clubs

the binding of feet

biohazards

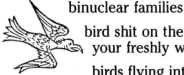

binuclear families

bird shit on the windshield of your freshly washed car

birds flying into windows

forgetting your birth control pills

birthdays

grotesque birthmarks

bitch, bitch, bitch

biting the hand that feeds you

biting off more than you can chew

biting your tongue

bitter cold

the bitter end

bizarre unions

blabbermouths

black and blue marks as they start turning green, yellow, and purple black holes

black market babies

blackouts

being the black sheep of the family

the Black Sox

black tie parties

the blahs

Lt. Colonel Henry Blake's death

blaming the victim

when there is no one to blame but yourself

drawing a blank

having your security blanket stolen

bleached blondes

blemishes

people who dress in one color of varying
shades that blend from head to toe

Captain Bligh

the blind leading the blind

blind dates

EVEN WORSE: when your blind date turns
out to be your ex-spouse

blockheads

block parties

bad blood

blood spurting all over you

high blood pressure

blood, sweat, and tears

blooper shows on TV

a blow to the head

trying to blow up a large, inflatable toy

blowfish

blowing your stack

coming to blows

trouble from out of the blue

singing the blues

blue balls

Bluebeard

blue noses

having your bluff called

when the past year is all a blur

boa constrictors

board meetings

boat people

bodybuilders

body counts

 body odor

losing an important body part

body snatchers

the bogeyman

having a boil lanced

boll weevils

bollixing things up

defusing a bomb

being thrown a bone

bongo drums

being booed off the stage

booby traps

boogers

book banning

when the last chapter of a mystery is torn out of the book

chain bookstores

bookends that are not strong enough to hold the books between them

miniature books

book reports

a bookstore burning down

bookstores that won't special order

boomerangs

Lizzie Borden

boredom

Robert Bork

having an accident in a borrowed car

borrowed books that are never returned

a boss who passes off your ideas as his or her own

having an affair with the boss's wife

turning to the bottle

the bottom of the barrel

the bottom line

bottomless pits

bouffant hairdos

realizing you can be bought

bouncing off the walls

catching the bouquet

bourgeois affectation

boutiques

questions from hospital personnel about your bowel movements

being bowlegged

professional bowling

boyfriends

falling asleep with the TV on and waking up to the Bozo show

bras with underwires that have poked out

having your braces tightened

the "Brady Bunch" theme song

brains (as food)

"The brain is an organ of minor importance."— Aristotle

feeling like your brain is going to explode

the sudden occupation of your brain by obsessive, irrational thoughts at the precise moment you would otherwise drop off to sleep

having your brake lines cut

spoiled brats

Eva Braun

bravado

barroom brawls

brazen hussies

bread lines

breaches of the public trust

waiting for your big break

break dancing

somebody breaking a record you set

going to someone's house and breaking an
irreplaceable family heirloom

 breaking a mirror

breaking up

not having enough time for a
nutritious breakfast

jogging with improper breast support

sagging breasts

wasting your breath

heavy breathing on the other end of the phone

Yul Brenner's anti-smoking commercial

bribery

bricks thrown through your window

people whose bridal gowns still fit on their twentieth wedding anniversaries

bridesmaids' dresses

the brig

people who don't turn their brights down when other cars are on the road

the brink of disaster

those who are too big for their britches

peanut brittle sticking to your teeth

being stone cold broke

broken bones

broken hearts

brooders

buying the Brooklyn Bridge

bromidrosiphobia: the abnormal fear of personal odor

the Bronx

brothels

brothers

being your brother's keeper

brush fires

Brussels sprouts

brownnosing

a bruised ego

walls painted with uneven brush strokes

brutal honesty

having bubble gum bubbles break all over your face

people who try to distract the guards at Buckingham Palace

the federal budget

budget motels

having a bug fly up your nose

building code violations

bulbs that don't bloom

Bulgaria

biting the bullet

bullet holes

the school bully

bumbling crooks

"I brake for _____" bumper stickers

people who have bumper stickers on their beaten up old cars that say "my other car is a Porsche"

people bumping into you

bunco artists

bunions

people who never got Archie Bunker

"There's three moments in a man's life: when he buys a house, a car, and a new color TV. That's what America is all about."—Archie Bunker

bearing the burden of another's discontent

bureaucrats

burial plots

being buried alive

a designer dress that looks like a burlap sack

a burning sensation in your chest

burning the midnight oil

burning out

being burned by steam when removing the cover of something cooked in the microwave burp guns

George Bush

taking care of business

business lunches

busy signals

people who refuse to move back on crowded buses

standing at a bus stop in the rain and having someone drive by and splash you

business trips

having business dealings with your ex

the shootout at the end of *Butch Cassidy and the Sundance Kid*

being the butt of a joke

"the butler did it"

buttinskis

needing five buttons but only finding four that match

sewing buttonholes that are too small for the buttons

buying tampons from a teenage, male salesperson

buzzards

tiny buzzing bugs you can hear but not see

buzzwords

cab drivers who don't speak English

Cabbage Patch Dolls

cabin fever

having the cable go out during the Superbowl

cable TV repair people

caffeine

speckled caymen

cake with too much frosting

"Calamities are of two kinds: misfortune to ourselves, and good fortune to others."— Ambrose Bierce

calcium deficiency

calculus

calculating money grubbers

pocket calendars that don't fit into your pockets

"California black tie"

the California Raisins

calling 911

call waiting

being called, "one of those left-wing, radical, hippie types" by a right-wing, radical, fascist type

people who call you "hon"

calories

the calm before the storm

Cambodia

camouflaged trucks in the city

campers who don't leave nature as they found it

being boiled by cannibals

the cancellation of "Mary Hartman, Mary Hartman"

cancer

cancer-causing agents in the ecosphere

burning the candle at both ends

gag candles that won't blow out

the thought of John Candy in a tutu

candystripers coming to bother you when you are in the hospital licking cane toads in order to get high off their hallucinogenic secretions

when the candidate you really believe in and have worked for loses

being shot out of a cannon

an empty canteen in the desert

the people who have been put to death for capital crimes, and were later found to be innocent

capriciousness

twist-off caps that don't twist off

being captured by the enemy

car dealers' commercials

cars that are faster than yours

cars that are slower than yours

cars that park across two (or more) parking spaces

an exciting career in carcass removal

the card catalogue

marked cards

the Phoenix Cardinals and Indianapolis Colts

cardsharps

"I care for no man on earth, and no man on earth cares for me."—Sydney Carton in *A Tale of Two Cities*

people who do not care

pretending not to care about anything

your career

carnal knowledge

carnivorous butterflies

Christmas caroling

grinding cookie crumbs into the carpet

getting carried away

carrion beetles

putting the cart before the horse

when Rick tells Ilsa to leave at the end of *Casablanca* and she does

Casey Casem

a repairperson casing your house

dropping your watch into an open casket

EVEN WORSE: getting it out

cashiers who can't make change

the caste system

castration

being clawed in the face by your cat

the smell of cat food

cat hair

drowned kittens

your cat landing on your chest in the middle of the night

when your cat proudly presents you with dead rodents

CAT scans

cataclysmic clouds of radioactive dust

Catch-22

catechisms

being catheterized

Catholicism

catching a hockey puck in your teeth

getting caught

being caught with your hand in the cookie jar

getting your head caught in an airplane propeller

getting caught with your pants down

being caught in the crossfire

getting caught singing aloud to the car radio

cauliflower ear

the cause célèbre

words of caution

caveat emptor

cavities

cracking ceilings

celibacy

tell-all celebrity books

cellulite

family members arguing over cemetery plots

censorship

the Center for Disease Control

centipedes

chain letters

chain smoking

sitting on a chair and having it break

not getting off the chairlift in time

trying to clean chalkboard erasers

the *Challenger* explosion

chamber pots

champagne bubbles up your nose

having only one chance

change

"subject to change without notice"

other people trying to change you

channeling

having hundreds of TV channels and still finding nothing good to watch

chaos

order

"Cat's in the Cradle" by Harry Chapin

Graham Chapman's death

Chapter Eleven

being charged more when they leave things out

that sinking feeling that the people leading you do not have a clue as to what they are doing

Flowers for Algernon

having your boss chase you around the desk

cheap shots

cheaters

"the check's in the mail"

when your checkbook *almost* balances, but is off by some odd amount like thirty-seven cents

checkbook charity

checking the baby every five minutes to make sure it is still breathing

being cheered up

cheerleaders

chemical additives

chemical warfare

Cher

Chernobyl

green maraschino cherries

slow chess players

being chewed out

Chia Pets

"tres chic"

the Chicago Cubs

counting your chickens before they are
hatched

chicken pox

chickens running around with
their heads cut off

"A chicken salad sandwich on toast, hold the
chicken salad." (*Five Easy Pieces*)

chiggers

chihuahuas

child actors

when your child does the exact thing you just
told him or her not to do

unresolved childhood difficulties

child snatchers

children

"Nobody": who your child was
talking to

"Nowhere": where your child is
going

"I dunno": what your child
knows

telling your children where babies come from

When your child tells you at 12:37 A.M. that he/she needs four empty salad dressing bottles, two cans of lychee nuts, six rolls of paper towels, and a spool of chartreuse thread to take to school at 6:45 A.M. or else he/she will be immediately expelled.

that Julia Child, the "French Chef," is from rural Odell, Illinois

breaking china of a pattern that has been discontinued

the chip on your shoulder

creamed chipped beef on toast

Chippendale dancers

chlamydia

chlorofluorocarbons

that chocolate has calories

people who bite into all of the chocolates and then put them back in the box

having no choice

the choices you've made

cholesterol

choosing the wrong parents

chopping onions

"Chopsticks"

a rousing chorus of "One Hundred Bottles of Beer on the Wall"

artificial Christmas trees

Christmas trees already decorated and delivered from catalogues

breaking your very favorite Christmas tree ornament

chromosomal abnormalities

chromatophobia: the irrational fear of colors

chronic fatigue syndrome

chumps

"Broadly speaking, human beings may be divided into three classes: those who are billed to death, those who are worried to death, and those who are bored to death."—Winston Churchill

the CIA

cibophobia: the irrational fear of food

cicadas

cigarette burns

cigarettes

going around in circles

adult circumcision

circumstantial evidence

circulatory diseases

being a victim of circumstance

being an ordinary person in an extraordinary circumstance

fighting city hall

city slickers

having your civil liberties violated

the end of civilization as we know it

"We are born princes, and the civilizing process turns us into frogs."—Eric Berne

bad clams

clandestine meetings

the class clown

classical tragedy

spring cleaning

when the dry cleaner ruins your favorite sweater

clearing the air

"The world seems to be a complete madhouse with [only] occasional pockets of serenity."—John Cleese

store clerks who don't know where anything
is in the store

the Cleveland Indians

clichés

having clients who don't take your advice

having a show cancelled during the summer,
after the cliff-hanger episode

clinophobia: the irrational fear of going
to bed

cloak and dagger work

getting clobbered

broken clocks

trying to get all of your clocks exactly
synchronized to the correct time

A Clockwork Orange

clogged gutters

closed meetings

coming out of the closet

kids closing themselves in abandoned
freezers and suitcases

the closing of your favorite store

closing on opening night

fans ripping the clothes off stars

black, ominous clouds

cloying sweetness

Club Med

not having a clue

clutching in an emergency

your coach

walking over hot coals

working in the coal mines

co-dependents

cocaine

      drinking a cockroach

    forgetting to plug the coffee pot in

  bad coffee

EVEN WORSE: cold coffee

THE WORST: no coffee

sleazy morticians who convince poor people
they need expensive coffins for their dead
loved ones

coffin nails

Roy Cohn

accidentally putting a hot beverage into a cold cup

the common cold

stepping onto a cold floor in the morning

cold showers

the cold shoulder

the Cold War

coincidence

collages

"collateral damage" (the military term for enemy civilian casualties)

college tuition

someone calling collect from Botswana

colloquialisms

cheap cologne

colorblindness

all the different shades of any one color

colorizing old movies

EVEN WORSE: colorizing *Casablanca*

colostomy bags

having your newspaper drop a columnist you really like

forgetting the combination to a lock

unfunny comedians

your comeuppance

not being able to find a comfortable position

when the feathers come out of your down comforter

douche commercials

how all TV stations play their commercials at the same time so you can't flip to another show during the commercial of the show you are watching

EVEN WORSE: that stations never break into commercials with important bulletins, only into programs

"I'm not a doctor, but I play one on TV."

trying to figure out why people with ring around the collar problems can't just wash their necks

the Snuggle Bear

when good songs are made into commercials

getting paid on commission

commitment

commitment hearings

communes

losing communication with the control tower

comparing your children to other children

ruthless competition

complacency in a relationship

managing to make the simplest things complex

complications

backhanded compliments

compost heaps

being in a compromising situation

compulsiveness

computers

computer dating services

computerese

computer viruses

Conan the Barbarian

people who don't go to concerts to hear the music

when you are too old for rock concerts

concession speeches

forgone conclusions

walking onto wet concrete

concubines

condemned buildings

a condom with a patch on it

the Confederacy

conference calls

confessing to a crime you did not commit

confidence games

conformists

being confounded by your enemies

people who confuse the D.U.I. issue with drinking alcohol at all

confusing what you do with who you are

confusion of the real with the ideal

conglomerates

conjugal duties

the consequences

consciousness expansion

ultraconservatism

consolation prizes

conspiracy

tampering with the Constitution

walking by a construction site if you're a woman

road construction

conspicuous consumption

losing a contact in shag carpeting

looking for signs that someone who has died is trying to contact you

yunky gunk collecting on the edges of food containers

cotangents

contemplating suicide

contortions

contraband

contract disputes

having a contract out on your life

messy contracts

contradictions

your spouse contradicting you in public

control freaks

doubling on eleven and drawing an ace

convalescent hospitals

accidentally having your long-saved-for dream vacation in a hotel with a bunch of conventioneering dentists

convenience store burritos

long-winded conversations

trying to get your convertible top up after it has already started to rain

being convicted with false evidence

standing up for your convictions

cooties

people who can't cope

crooked cops

good cop/bad cop

copperheads

coprostasophobia: the irrational fear of constipation

copycat killings

"The inability to slam cordless phones"— Jerry Seinfeld

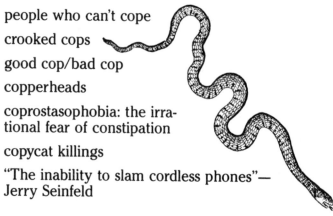

soggy cornflakes

cornball movies that make you cry

corporate America

people who constantly correct you

corrosion

Bill Cosby movies

the cosmos

the cost of children's shoes

the high cost of living

cost analyses

the couch stuffing coming out

a raspy cough

coughing so hard your ribs break

the countdown before a bomb detonation

counterfeit money

countries where children don't receive immunizations

countries where people eat dogs

restricted country clubs

a coup

lacking courage

being ripped to pieces in court

when the person you are in bed with steals all of the covers

cover girls

coverups

U.S. covert actions

gooshy cowpies stuck to your tent

howling coyotes

crab grass

cracking the spine of a valuable book

cracking sounds as you bend at the knee

crackpots

cracking up

cramming

trying to find cranberry juice without other fruits in it

crass commercialism

Joan Crawford

Crayola retiring eight "classic" colors

dealing with crazy people in public places

cream puffs

the creative process

not giving yourself enough credit

credit cards

EVEN WORSE: trying to reverse a bad credit rating

crematoriums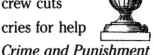

crew cuts

cries for help

Crime and Punishment

crimes against nature

coming home and finding that yellow "crime scene" ribbon around your house

crime waves

a crisis of conscience

that everyone is a critic

self-criticism

crossbreeding

inadvertently trying to pick up a cross dresser

crossword puzzles

Jim Crow laws

crowds

the creeping crud

cruel and unusual punishment

the cruelty of strangers

cruising

the Crusades

having a crush

people who crush beer cans on their foreheads

EVEN WORSE: people crushing beer cans on *your* forehead

crutches

cryogenics

crypts

a clouded crystal ball

cubism

sinking the cue ball

cult classics

cultural imperialism

culture shock

colored cummerbunds

having a curfew

curiosity

torn curtains

curve balls

anyone that kills a curve

custody battles

going through customs

that the customer has gone from always right
to never right

cutting your losses

cuts on joints that have to move

cyanide

cyclones

D-Day

daddy longlegs

damp firewood

damnation

damned if you do, damned if you don't

the Sword of Damocles

damsels in distress

dance lessons

imminent danger

Rodney Dangerfield

dangling participles

daredevils

being left in the dark

the powers of darkness

someone opening the door of your darkroom

darning socks

the first Darren on "Bewitched"

dashed hopes

data entry

blind dates

first dates

your date leaving with someone else

when your date says he'll call and never does

New Year's Eve without a date

day-glo colors

having the daylights knocked out of you

The Day the Music Died

people who keep dead bodies in bags in the freezer

finding a dead body

having the government declare you dead

when you put lots of money into a slot machine, don't win anything, and finally walk away, only to have the next person win a huge jackpot on their first quarter

near-death experiences

a fate worse than death

the suddenly nice things people say about the creep who just died

"Death always comes too early or too late."—English proverb

death threats

"Until death do us part"

death row

looking like death warmed over

having a death wish

the debasement of women

debating on behalf of a position you don't personally believe in

debt

decadence

decapitation

decisions, decisions, decisions

people who refuse to make decisions about *anything*

decomposed bodies

decoys

obnoxious deejays

defeat

structural defects in airplanes

making definite pronouncements that turn out to be wrong

being deferential

vitamin deficiency

deficit spending

different definitions for the same word in different dictionaries

deforestation

defrosting the freezer

being degraded

dehumanization

dehydration

delay tactics

accidentally deleting all of your files

Deliverance

when the newspaper delivery person tosses the paper into the bushes

juvenile delinquents

having the wrong furniture delivered

waiting at home all day for a delivery that doesn't arrive

paranoid delusions

endless demands

the Democrats

demagogues

demolition derbies

demonic possession

trying to make the demons go away

when your parents turn your old room into a den

Dennis the Menace

Denny's

finding greatest common denominators

dentists who ask you questions when they have their hands in your mouth

dental instruments

people who use cologne in place of deodorant

deportation

depravity

depression

the desire to watch really depressing movies when you are already, in fact, quite depressed

the Great Depression

sensory deprivation tanks

dereliction of duty

the desecration of headstones

when each member of your party thinks someone else is the designated driver

the designated hitter

designer jeans

not being able to see the top of your desk

desolation

desperados

quiet desperation

"To know all is not to forgive all. It is to despise everybody."—Quentin Crisp

despots

just desserts

mass destruction

a date with destiny

destitution

destrophobia: the abnormal fear of turning right

being destroyed by your past

sketchy detail

detention

detours

deviant sexual behavior

standard deviations

diabetes

an incorrect diagnosis

diagramming sentences

a flawed diamond

Dianetics

leaky diapers

73

being unable to get your diaphragm out

verbal diarrhea

loaded dice

diatribes

when you can't find a word in the dictionary because you can't spell it

poor diction

"The best way to get praise is to die."—Italian proverb

diets

fearing people who are racially, socially, economically, or religiously different from you

digging yourself into a hole

digestion

dim bulbs

diminishing returns

people who say "din-din"

that all the dinosaurs are gone

Diner

being sent to bed without dinner

dinner parties

dioxin

diplomatic immunity

direct-mail advertising

dirt

dirty old men

disappearing without a trace

disappointing the one person whose opinion you really care about

knowing that someone secretly disapproves of you

a state of disbelief

severe disciplinarians

disclaimers

disco

the winter of your discontent

being discredited

discrimination

disenchantment

doing the dishes

dishonorable discharges

disillusionment

disinformation

disintegration

disliking your best friend's significant other

a dislocated shoulder

I Dismembered Mama

disobeying a direct order

disorderly conduct

disorientation

feeling as though you are disposable

disruption

writing your dissertation

dissidents

dissipation

"Distance: the only thing that the rich are willing for the poor to call theirs and keep."—Ambrose Bierce

hotel housekeepers who ignore "do not disturb" signs

little ditties

a diva with laryngitis

accidentally diving into shallow water

division

dizzy broads

"Do as I say, not as I do"

"Do you want to talk about it?"

"doing" lunch

doing the same thing every day

discovering your doctor never went to medical school

doctors with AIDS

a doctor with no bedside manner

docudramas

setting your VCR to tape a three hour documentary on Sigmund Freud and getting three hours of the Three Stooges instead

documents that require you to sign them with witnesses

not having the proper documents for an audit

dodgeball

dodging bullets

seeing doe eyes in your headlights

abandoned puppies on the side of the road

attack dogs

one dog barking in the neighborhood, and setting off a whole chain
of barking dogs for miles around

the *second* time your dog bites someone

dogs left alone in hot cars, with the windows
closed

being dog tired

walking the dog, at night, in the rain

dolls with heads that bob

dolls with their heads pulled off

the plight of the dolphins

domestic disturbances

domination

the domino effect

wondering why Donald Duck wears a shirt
but no pants

Don Juans

"What's done is done"

convenience store doughnuts

doomsayers

doomsday

people who want to censor "Doonesbury"

opening your car door and stepping on a dead squirrel

squeaky door hinges

dorm life

dot-to-dots that don't work

having a double

double agents

double-checking

double chins

double crosses

double entendres

double jeopardy

leading a double life

the Dow-Jones

downtime

the downtrodden

downward mobility

first drafts

fire-breathing dragons

being dragged by a bus because you got your foot caught in the door dragging the river for bodies

hair clogging your drain

rips in your drapes

people who draw little hearts and smiley faces over their "i"s instead of dots

going back to the drawing board

being drawn and quartered

drawing the line

"I only dread one day at a time."—Charlie Brown

the impossible dream

waking up in the middle of a really great dream

dreaming that you are naked and lost in a public place

dreaming your own death

your parents' dreams for you

the dregs of humanity

finding the perfect dress. . .in the wrong size

trying to dress a squirming baby

people who dress their dogs

walking into a room where someone else is wearing your dress dribble glasses

drifting apart

drill sergeants

people who drink milk right from the carton

driveby shootings

being married, or significantly involved with someone who has a drastically different sex drive than you do

back-seat drivers

drunk drivers

driving across the country with someone who has drastically different music tastes than you do

people who drive on the shoulder during bumper to bumper traffic

seeing a driverless, moving car

drivers who don't signal

driving with someone who won't ask for directions

driving really far to a store to pick up something they told you they had and getting there only to be told the person on the phone was wrong and they actually don't have what you need at all

going practice driving with your child

being unable to hear at drive-in movies

driving the wrong way down a one-way street

 freezing drizzle

being dropped from the top of a 15-foot wall

dropping the ball

when you child drops out of life and goes to live in an ashram

dropsy

drought

drowning in flaming oil

a drowned puppy in your toilet bowl

drowning your troubles

drugs

random drug testing

the evil person who gave your child a set of drums

drunk passengers on airplanes

drunken sailors on leave

dry rot

dryers that eat only one sock

ducks as food

a deflated rubber ducky

due dates

paying your dues

David Duke

the doldrums

Dullsville

the dump

standing in the corner with a duncecap on

dung beetles

biting the dust

dynamiting fish

dysentery

sexual dysfunction

dystopias

E: none of the above

eager beavers

ceramic eagles

ears that are too big for your head

punctured ear drums

when your ears pop on airplanes and elevators

ear wax

having a pierced earring ripped out of your ear lobe

contemplating what would happen if the earth were to be hit by a giant asteroid

"Animals, which move, have limbs and muscles, the earth has no limbs and muscles, hence it does not move."—Scipio Chiaramonti

being buried during an earthquake

earwigs

that which is easier said than done

Easter bunny stew

eating when you are not hungry

eating your words

people who can eat anything without gaining an ounce

eccentricities

staring into a total eclipse

people who make fortunes destroying our economy

edicts

the cutting edge

teetering precariously on the edge

being edgy

the Edsel

last ditch efforts

cracking eggs into a bowl full of other ingredients, and having one of them be bad

egg on your face

that moment of tension right after you've been tossed an egg at the annual egg toss

ego trips

Adolf Eichmann

being behind the eight ball

eight track tapes

"Einstein has not a logical mind."—Jeremiah J. Callahan, President of Duquesne University

El Salvador

tennis elbow

elections

the Electra complex

electric cattle prods

if your job is pulling the lever to activate the electric chair

the electric company

being wrong when you thought you turned the electricity off before doing some repair work

electrolysis

battling the elements

getting on an elevator where the button for every floor is pushed

people who press the elevator button repeatedly

elevator shoes

Elvis impersonators

embalming fluid

dying of embarrassment

embezzlement

tests of the Emergency Broadcasting System

emergency rooms

being in an emergency room staffed with a group of new interns mixed emotions

filling that empty space inside with Twinkies

a walking encyclopedia who won't shut up

trying to make ends meet

reaching the end of your rope

endangered animals

the enemy

archenemies

Public Enemy Number One

sleeping with the enemy

the enemy within

the Energizer rabbit

English food

when the head of the English department at your school goes home at night, dons a weasel suit, and steals other people's chickens

people who come to live in America but refuse to learn English

EVEN WORSE: people in government offices who don't speak English

everything you really should have enjoyed, but didn't

ennui

entombment

missing your entrance

entrepreneurs

entropy

epidemics

epitaphs

losing your equilibrium

lack of pay equity for women

failure of the E.R.A

the inability to maintain an erection

placing last in a beauty contest

ergomania: the irrational need to work

eroding coastlines

erratic behavior

eruptions at the dinner table

escalators that don't run

espionage

EST

the establishment

anti-establishmentalists

estate planning

when you think E.T. is going to die at the hands of the government doctors

"What to come up and see my etchings?"

eunuchs

euphemisms for body parts

euphemisms for death

euthanasia

evasive public officials

tax evasion

child evangelists

everything

admissible evidence that works against you

EVEN WORSE: inadmissible evidence that works for you

evil

the evil eye

the lesser of two evils

evil spirits

"All the ills from which America suffers can be traced back to the teaching of evolution. It would be better to destroy every other book written, and save just the first three verses of Genesis."—William Jennings Bryant

exacerbating an affront

exam week

early morning exercise shows with peppy hosts

excessive demands

feeling excluded

excommunication

lame excuses

executing murderers to show that killing people is wrong

executioners

exerting yourself to the point of exhaustion

exhibitionism

contemplating that this day (minute, hour, year) will never exist again

living in exile

dead ends

having your tax refund become a "dead letter"

missing your deadline

while walking through a cemetery, realizing you are walking on dead people's heads

wondering if dead people can sit up

deadly force

D-Day

"Let's Make a Deal"

James Dean

"Dear John" letters

death

death bed requests

expectations: diminished, high, parental, unrealistic, *Great*

other people's expense accounts

"experts"

expiration dates

all of the things you can't explain

unacceptable explanations

exploding animals

exploring the inner self

explosions

people who go into the express line with more than ten items

extenuating circumstances

an exterminator who's afraid of bugs

extremists

people who are obnoxiously extroverted

Exxon

the eye of the storm

bloodshot eyes

"Life for life, eye for an eye, tooth for tooth, hand for hand, foot for foot."—*Leviticus*

having your eyes gouged out of their sockets

contaminated eye makeup

that icky gunk that collects in the corner of your eye

eyebrows that grow together

short eyelashes

"e-z"

face lifts

facing the music

a face only a mother could love

EVEN WORSE: a mother who doesn't love it

faded upholstery

fads

when people fail you

giving blood and being really cocky, and standing up too fast and fainting

your fifteen minutes of fame

failing a test

fainting at the sight of blood

when fair is foul

"all is fair in love and war"

lack of faith

fake I.D.s

fake orgasms

fallen idols

falling asleep on the beach and waking up with half your face sunburned

falling through a hole in the ice

fallout zones

being sold a false bill of goods

bearing false witness

Jerry Falwell

false hopes

families where all of the children have names that rhyme or start with the same letter

family farm foreclosures

family reunions

family traditions

famine

being the child of someone famous

farsightedness

farm smells

farting

going too fast

fast food chains

calculating your fat intake

fatal attractions

fatalism

fate

fathers

discovering the father of your baby is not who you thought it was

faucets that drip in the middle of the night

"A writer is congenitally unable to tell the truth and that is why we call what he writes fiction."—William Faulkner

those who find fault with everything

the San Andreas fault

a faux pas

junk fax

going on the F.B.I. tour

living in constant fear

confronting your worst fears

fearing your own success

the federal government

feeble attempts at humor

trying to feed a baby something it doesn't want to eat

feelings

EVEN WORSE: "Feelings"

causing someone you care for to feel bad

feeling blue

feeling hungover when you are not

feeling invisible

feeling like just another pebble on the beach

"If it feels good, do it"

having to do grownup things even though you feel like a kid inside

feeling like the whole world is judging you

not feeling like yourself

feeling ugly, used, touchy, unloved, unclean, numb, insecure, fat, or like a fool

cold feet

pig's feet

Fellini movies

feminine intuition

militant feminism

holes in your fence

sitting on the fence

Ferraris

fetid villages

fiduciary responsibility

fights breaking out between war supporters and peace supporters fighting like cats and dogs

fighting dirty

figures of speech

"I've found that evil usually triumphs, unless good is very, very careful."—Dr. Leonard "Bones" McCoy, on "Star Trek"

file drawers that slide off the rail

loose fillings

filling in the blanks

finals

financial ruin

finding something unrecognizable in your refrigerator

saying "I'm fine, thank you," when you aren't

the fine print

fingernails on a blackboard

breaking a nail

stapling your finger

the finish rubbing off

the Great Chicago Fire

imported fire ants

living next door to a fire department

fire drills

faulty fire extinguishers

forgetting to open the flue before you start a fire

playing with fire

being fired

EVEN WORSE: being arbitrarily fired

THE WORST: being arbitrarily fired on Christmas Eve, and then having to train a replacement for yourself

being on the wrong end of a firing squad

fireworks that fizzle

the first day of school

your first kiss

first love

the first time you have your new in-laws over to your home

the first time

 fish tank algae

cleaning fish

being served a fish with its head still on

reeling in a big fish and having the line break

trying to fit a square peg into a round hole

when your favorite jeans don't fit anymore

five o'clock shadow

when the fix is on

fixing things that are not broken

Colonel Flagg

your flambe catching the table on fire

flanking maneuvers

emergency flares that don't work

hot flashes

flashbacks

flashers

discovering your flashlight batteries are dead
during a power outage

being swayed by flattery

your own tragic flaw

dogs with fleas

fleeting romance

fruit flies

a fly in your ointment

a flywheel with missing teeth

flight delays

flimflams

your last fling

the flip side

flirting

flash floods

people who leave wet towels and dirty underwear on the bathroom floor

those rides at amusement parks where the walls spin and the floor drops out

buzzing fluorescent light bulbs

dead flowers

EVEN WORSE: artificial flowers

flower children

when the flu hangs on

EVEN WORSE: getting the flu from flu shots

fluffy news

flunking out of school

flying by the seat of your pants

driving through the mountains, at night, in the fog

old fogeys

EVEN WORSE: young fogeys

getting stuck in a fold-up bed

when your business folds

being followed

food in your beard

food you can't identify

being told to eat food you don't want "because of the starving children in India"

fools falling in love

pre-season football

going into a big game with your back-up quarterback

the NFL

the French playing American football

opening your mouth and inserting your foot

trying to keep track of foreign currency

the increasing foreign ownership of American land and natural resources foreign policy

not seeing the forest for the trees

that which takes forever and a day

forgetting

being forgotten

running into the person you forgot to invite to your party

bent tines on forks

formaldehyde

formula novels

fortune cookies

inadequate foster care

foul play

fragging

fragmentation grenades

being framed

franchising

Anne Frank

that nobody seems to realize that Frankenstein isn't a monster at all, but the person who *created* the monster

frantic holiday rushes

fraternities

fraud

when you're worn to a frazzle

freak shows

that the best things in life really aren't free

"If people have to choose between freedom and sandwiches, they will take sandwiches."
—Lord Boyd-Orr

freelance writing

the French

Freudian slips

fair weather friends

the first year all the friends you grew up with don't make it home for the holidays

frigidity

when your fridge is on the fritz

frivolous lawsuits

Squeaky Fromme

cold fronts

frostbite

"He's turned his life around. He used to be depressed and miserable, and now he's miserable and depressed."—David Frost

when Frosty the Snowman melts

frozen food that doesn't even remotely resemble the picture on the package

fruit on hats

frumps

fugitives from justice

hearing your *full* name being called by one of your parents

"Most of the time I don't have much fun. The rest of the time, I don't have any fun at all."—Woody Allen

religious fundamentalism

fundraisers

accidentally cutting into a funeral procession you are not a part of

no one showing up at your funeral

people who view funerals as parties

fungus

hitting your funny bone

the funny farm

the compulsion to rearrange all your furniture, and ending up with it all right back where you started

people who protect their furniture by not using it

blowing a fuse

fussy eaters

"The future is almost like the present, only longer."—Yogi Berra

the future of the human race

the gift of gab

Zsa Zsa Gabor

social gaffes

"In the end, everything is a gag."—Charlie Chaplin

gag gifts

gallows humor

gambling

EVEN WORSE: gambling and losing

taping a big game you were dying to watch, and having someone tell you the outcome before you get to see it

playing the game

game show hosts

missing a game piece

gamomania: the insane need to be married

gang colors

gangrene

generation gaps

gaps between your front teeth

the garbage truck at five in the morning

breaking the bottom of a full garbage bag

that Garfield used to be funny

that architects don't use gargoyles anymore

hitting the gas instead of the brake

spilling gas on your clothes and walking into
a room where there are lots of smokers

an empty gas tank

gate crashers

the gates of hell

gatekeepers

Jay Gatsby

circus geeks

Gordon Gekko

flawed gemstones

generalizations

genetic engineering

violations of the Geneva Convention

fruit-flavored genital sprays

genophobia: the abnormal fear of sex

geometry: algebraic, analytic, circle, denumerative, Euclidean, non-Euclidean, geodesic, hyperbolic, line, nilpoint, projective

Geraldo Rivera

the reunification of Germany

gerrymandering

empty gestures

Estelle Getty

ghettos

the Ghost of Christmas Past

ghost writers

G.I. Joe

seeing the gift you gave someone in the trash

gigolos

gila monsters

that the folks on Gilligan's Island can build
radios out of coconuts, but they can't build a
raft to take them off the island

gingivitis

Ginsu knife sets

girlfriends

girls popping out of cakes

give and take

giving up

gladhandling

glamorized names for mundane jobs

knowing the glass is half empty

scratched lenses

streaky glassware

glory hounds

sniffing glue

gluttony

the GNP

go-go boots

never reaching your goal

"Go ahead, make my day."—Dirty Harry

that almost anywhere you go, everything looks the same

trying to go home again

"God is dead"

"If God lived on earth, people would break his windows."— Yiddish proverb

gold diggers

swallowing live goldfish

gold lame jumpsuits

golf

all of the things you are not good at

finding Mr. Goodbar

when bad people get all the attention and when your goodness gets ignored

when you can't tell the good guys from the bad guys

"A good deed never goes unpunished"—Gore Vidal

when your local Good Humor man is a drug dealer

"It's for your own good"

"If it's good, they'll stop making it."—Herbert Block

good ol' boys

that all good things must come to an end

the goon squad

gossip

when everything is up for grabs

having to get a real job after graduation

graffiti

going against the grain

going too far

poor grammar

delusions of grandeur

telling your children's grandparents that you are leaving the children to someone other than them should both you and your spouse die

taking your partner for granted

The Grapes of Wrath

a cow grazing on your grass skirt

gratuitous violence

falling into an open grave

grave robbers

a graveside funeral service in the rain

the graveyard shift

falling and getting gravel in your cuts

lumpy gravy

gray areas

the GREs

forgetting to grease the pan

grease fires

Grecian Formula

greed

Greek tragedy

"Green Acres"

the greenhouse effect

the green-eyed monster

when the first friend of your age dies

the grim reaper

grinches

growing up

grubs

a big bowl full of gruel

gruesome endings

rotten guacamole

guano

an armed guard at your office

Bob Guccione

guerilla warfare

second guessing

high school guidance counselors

guilt

guilty people who are acquitted

Poor Gwenhwyfar, kept apart from Lancelet

the Gulf War

bleeding gums

Bryant Gumbel

kids carrying guns to school

"cop killer" bullets

"Guns don't kill people, people kill people."

guppies devouring their babies

"Nothing so needs reforming as other people's habits."—Mark Twain

hackysacks

when you've absolutely had it

old hags

bad haircuts

hairy backs

"big hair" babes

mistaking hairspray for deodorant

halitosis

making an elaborate Halloween costume for your child and having him/her refuse to wear it

the year you don't find Halloween haunted houses scary anymore

hallucinations

Hamburger Helper

when your face looks like hamburger meat

someone hammering when you are trying to think

pulled hamstrings

living hand to mouth

brown spots on your hands

when your hands are tied

illegible handwriting

"hang in there"

hangnails

happy-go-lucky types

a book of things to be happy about

"Happiness: an agreeable sensation arising
from contemplating the misery of another."—
Ambrose Bierce

things which made you happy as a child, but
now make you miserable as an adult

"My friends know that to me happiness is
when I am merely miserable and not
suicidal."—Bob Fosse

happy people

harboring a fugitive

doing things the hard way

harebrained schemes

Hare Krishnas

Harlequin Romances

when the person who harms you gets off
with a slap on the wrist

when no one will believe Harvey is real

a has-been at twenty

haste

sitting behind someone wearing a tall hat at the theater

burying the hatchet

EVEN WORSE: a hatchet buried in your skull

accepting hate and rejecting love

if somebody up there hates you

"Few people can be happy unless they hate some other person, nation, or creed."— Bertrand Russell

haughtiness

hauling off and hitting someone

being haunted by your past

Harvard MBAs

"Have a nice day"

having nothing to wear

Hawaiian shirts

hay fever

searching for a needle in a haystack

transporting hazardous materials

bumping your head on the car door

heads you win, tails I lose

splitting headaches

headhunters

head lice

being served your head on a platter

head shops

hearing things

"Heartbreak Hotel"

bleeding hearts

your heart's desire

"Hearts will never be practical until they can be made unbreakable."—The Tin Man in *The Wizard of Oz*

heartburn

Heart of Darkness

wearing your heart on your sleeve

prickly heat

the old heave-ho

"heavy metal"

hecklers

hedging your bets

hedonophobia: the abnormal fear of pleasure

the heebie jeebies

"Hee Haw"

breaking a heel

saving some stranger in a restaurant from choking by performing the Heimlich maneuver and then being sued for breaking his/her ribs

Hugh Hefner

hellfire

Hell's Angels

Jesse Helms

unhelpful help

people who need help but can't get it

Helter Skelter

"If two people love each other, there can be no happy end to it."—Ernest Hemingway

big hemorrhoids

Jim Henson's death

heredity

heretics

the lack of heroes

hesitation

"hey, dude"

everybody's cures for the hiccups

painful hickeys

having nowhere to hide

hidden agendas

hideous freaks of nature

office hierarchy

the high cost of living

high school dropouts

high school reunions

high-voltage fences

hiking for nine hours uphill in one hundred degree heat only to realize you've made a complete circle

hindsight

hissing and booing

"History is merely gossip."—Oscar Wilde

history repeating itself

rewritten history

being hit below the belt

hit-and-run drivers

"What luck for the rulers that men do not think."—Adolf Hitler

hitting the books

hoaxes

hobgoblins

hockey brawls

being hoisted by your own petard

the hokey pokey

people calling you and then putting you on hold

holding back

holding out

a hole in your head

hole punchers that make cockeyed holes

holidays apart from the one you love

Buddy Holly's death

the embarrassment you feel when you're fooled by a hologram

home economics

the demolition of your childhood home

homelessness

homeless children worried that Santa can't
find them

home repair

the Home Shopping Network

if the dog *really does* eat your homework

homicidal maniacs

homonyms

that honesty is not *always* the best policy

"honey," "sweetie," or "baby"

people who honk when traffic is completely
stalled and there is no place to go

the honor code

hooligans

Mr. Hooper's death

J. Edgar Hoover

Bob Hope

hopelessness

hormones

a stuck car horn

running into a hornet's nest

horoscopes

horses with broken legs

horseplay (it's fun "until someone gets hurt")

when the hospital mixes up the babies

hospital food

those horrible hospital gowns that don't close in the back

being in the hospital with a roommate who has lots of loud, annoying visitors

hostile takeovers

cold nights in lonely hotels

the hotel losing your reservation while they are having a convention

hot pants

your hour of need

house arrest

housekeepers who answer the phone but don't speak English

house sales you must pay an admission fee to get into

noises from your house settling

the House Unamerican Activities Committee

housing developments with ridiculous names

housing projects

hucksters

HUD

human bites

the human condition

trying to change human nature

coming in last in the human race

"human remains pouches" (the military term for body bags)

humble pie

humidity

the most humiliating experience of your life

Hummel figurines

trying to make it to hump day

Humpty Dumpty

sitting hunched over for long periods of time

hunters accidentally shooting each other

when you are really, really sick, but they can't find anything wrong with you

having to give a stool sample

when all is said and done

hurricanes

being hurt by someone you love

EVEN WORSE: hurting the one you love

a nagging husband

Saddam Hussein

hydrophobia: the abnormal fear of water

hype

hyperactive children

not getting enough fun out of life

hypochondriacs

hypnophobia: the irrational fear of sleep

hypocrisy

hypodermic needles washing up on the shores

the performance of unnecessary hysterectomies

taking both positions so you can say "I told you so"

ICBMs

finding empty ice cube trays in the freezer

not eating ice cream fast enough to keep it in the cone

picking up dry ice with your bare hands

ice picks

icy roads

ichthyomania: the abnormal excitement about fish

an identity crisis

idiosyncracies

ignorance

ignoring people

iguanas

ill-gotten gains

illicit love affairs

illiteracy

doing things in an illogical order

figments of your imagination

imitation anything

immigration and naturalization

immutability

imperfection

Imperialist pigs

feeling as though you are impersonating a grownup

hair implants

having nothing important to say

people who tell you they don't want to impose on you as they do exactly that

the impossible and the improbable

impotence

first impressions

an appearance of impropriety

impulse buying

impure thoughts

an overflowing in box

your own inabilities

other people's inabilities

the inability to identify and label your feelings

inaccuracy

incantations

incessant jabbering

inchoate fears

all those "in-" words: incompetence, inconstancy, incontinence, incompatibility, incredulousness, incongruence, incommensuration, inconclusiveness, incomprehensibility, indecency, indecisiveness, indecorousness, indifference, indigestion, indignities, indiscretion, inebriation, inefficiency, inequities, infamy, infidelity, infertility, inflexibility, ingrates, inhumanity, injustice, insanity, insipidness, and insincerity

incurable diseases

indentured servitude

when the people you work with consider you indispensable

indexes that don't list subjects under any word you would ever think to look under

infectious diseases

inferiority complexes

Dante's *Inferno*

infinity

split infinitives

inflammatory statements

inflatable women

inflation

bad influences

good influences

paid informants

"infomercials"

having started making a recipe and then discovering you're out of one of the ingredients

ingrown toenails

smeared ink

borrowing money from your in-laws

"There is no such thing as inner peace. There is only nervousness and death."—Fran Liebowitz

loss of innocence

innuendo

the Spanish Inquisition

insecticide

insider trading

people insisting you did something
you didn't

insomnia

insurmountable odds

installment payments

instant replay

doing something against your better instincts

insults to your intelligence

adding insult to injury

insurance salespeople

not going to the hospital when you're in
trouble because you don't have insurance

the number of people who have integrity

neonatal intensive care units

the best of intentions

interior decorators

internal injuries

1–800–829–1040 (the IRS)

interrogations

introductions

intruders

inventing something wonderful that no one will take seriously

being invaded

bad investments

receiving an invitation after the party is over

unwittingly becoming involved

IOUs

IRA terrorists

Iran

Iraq

too many irons in the fire

an iron fist in a velvet glove

irreconcilable differences

irregularity

that which is irrelevant and immaterial

"There is only what is."—Lenny Bruce

that which is

that which isn't

that which might be

that which never will be

It's a Wonderful Life

itching under your cast

itinerant workers

the "It's a Small World" ride at Disneyland

ivory

living in an ivory tower

Iwo Jima

a short left jab

the jabberwocky

jackboots

jackhammering

Jack the Ripper

trying to fix your Jaguar

trying to fix a jaguar

"Do not pass go, do not collect two hundred dollars."

forgetting to put cell doors on the new jail

not being able to get jars open

jargon

clenching your jaw

jealousy

Dr. Jekyll and Mr. Hyde

buttered popcorn-flavored jellybeans

knowing all of the answers when watching "Jeopardy"

"Drop Kick Me Jesus Through the Goal Posts of Life" by Bobby Bare

jet lag

jet-setters

putting together a twenty-five hundred piece jigsaw puzzle of a landscape, getting to the end, and having one piece missing

jingoism

a jinx

The Book of Job

hating your job

job interviews

having to spend lots of money to find a new job, which you wouldn't be looking for in the first place if you had enough money from your old job

jock itch

running without a jock strap

joint custody

ethnic jokes

inside jokes you don't get

telling a joke, getting to the end, and forgetting the punchline

the Jolly Roger

Jolt Cola

a visit to Davy Jones's locker

Jim Jones

trying to keep up with the Joneses

journalistic gaffes

Judaism

judging a book by its cover

judgmental psychotherapists

corrupt judges

juggling too many responsibilities

jumping through hoops

having someone jump down your throat

the law of the jungle

being a "junior"

junior high

junk bonds

junk food

being called for jury duty and going and sitting in an airless, smoke-filled room all day, and never being called, or even spoken to by anyone all day

"just this once"

justice

the end justifying the means

"The meaning of life is that it stops."—Franz Kafka

kainotophobia: the abnormal fear of anything new

kamikazes: the drinks and the planes

bad karma

kathiosophobia: the irrational fear of sitting down

"keep in touch"

an empty keg

the picture of John F. Kennedy, Jr. saluting the casket of his father

"One fifth of the people are against everything all of the time."—Robert F. Kennedy

being kept

how Miss Piggy treats Kermit

people who put ketchup on everything

breaking off part of your key in the lock

spilling Coke on your keyboard

Genghis Khan

the Khmer Rouge

a kick in the pants

selling your kidney

really cute little kids on irritating TV commercials

when your child decides to throw a really big tantrum in the middle of a crowded department store, and everyone stares at you as though you are committing child abuse

hearing yourself talk to your children the way your parents spoke to you

when your children tear the labels off the canned goods

kidnapping the wrong person

Don King

the assassination of Martin Luther King, Jr.

Søren Kierkegaard

Henry Kissinger

the kiss of death

kids getting into the cabinet under the kitchen sink

kinked telephone cords

the Ku Klux Klan

kleptomania

banging your knees under the table

knee-jerk reactions

scrubbing the floor on your hands and knees

having your kneecaps broken

if you only knew then what you know now

knick-knacks

when your knight in shining armor rusts

someone knocking over your sandcastle

knocking over a huge display in a crowded grocery store

trying to get very tiny, tightly pulled knots out

people who don't know what they are doing

135

"Don't I know you from somewhere?"

"Do you come here often?"

"'Know thyself?' If I knew myself, I'd run away."— Goethe

knowing something terrible is about to happen

cracking knuckles

Ted Koppel's hair

wanting to keep kosher, but having a true love for pork

KP duty

Mrs. Kravitz on "Bewitched"

Kryptonite

"attention K-Mart shoppers"

kung fu movies

being labelled

being reminded to breathe while in labor

heavy physical labor

labyrinths

a rousing game of lacrosse

flimsy ladders

laissez-faire

being on the lam

lame ducks

wearing a lampshade on your head

faulty landing gear

the amount of landfill space being taken up by disposable diapers

landslides

crumbling landmarks

people who can't pick a lane

"Lane ends, merge left" during evening rush hour in a strange city

Laos

the College of Laputa

Lyndon Larouche

lasciviousness

Las Vegas

eighty lashes with a wet noodle

lashing out at the ones you love

the last dance

Edith Bunker's death

when your last resort fails

the last straw

knowing this is the last time you will ever see someone

people who are always late

EVEN WORSE: waiting for someone who is *never* late the *one* time they are

laughing to keep from crying

being laughed at

laugh tracks

people who can't laugh at themselves

being laughed at by lingerie salespeople when you try things on

dirty laundry strewn all over the floor

having your clothes snatched from the laundromat

hot molten lava

"Laverne and Shirley"

unconstitutional laws

taking the law into your own hands

lawn jockeys

138

lawyers

laxative abuse

unscheduled layovers

a lead balloon

lead paint

learning as you go along

Timothy Leary

trying to get out of your lease

children on leashes

leather skirts

people who won't leave you alone

leaving a trail of blood

Lebanon

blood sucking leeches

being left at the altar

being left-handed and sitting at a right-handed school desk

bird legs

being unable to get your legs cleanly shaven

people who will go to any lengths to get what they want

lime-green leisure suits

lemmings

"If life gives you lemons, make lemonade."

lending someone your bike, and having it be stolen while they have it

lending money to friends

John Lennon's death

giving up Judaism for Lent

trying to get a leopard to change its spots

leopard skin pants

leper colonies

the waters of Lethe

lethal injections

irrational silent letters, like the g and k in "knight"

letting other people down

letting go

frozen lettuce

leveraged buyouts

Jerry Lewis

"I have so much on my mind, and yet so little to say."—Richard Lewis

good liars

Liberace

Libya

high school librarians

overdue library books

chewing lice

having your driver's license revoked

the fact that you need a license to drive a car but not to have a baby

people who lick their fingers and then stick them back into something

lie detectors

the great lies of history

discovering the lies your parents told you

life

"For the unhappy man death is the commutation of a sentence of life imprisonment."—Alexander Chase

"Life is anything that dies when you stomp on it."—Dave Barry

trying to figure out what to do with your life

when the only thing you are ever optimistic about is pessimism

"life plus ninety-nine years"

when life passes you by

"Life as we find it is too hard for us; it entails too much pain, too many disappointments, impossible tasks."—Sigmund Freud

"Life is a gamble at terrible odds, if it was a bet you wouldn't take it."—Tom Stoppard

punctured life rafts

"Lifestyles of the Rich and Famous"

people who think they know more about your life than you do

burned-out light bulbs

being struck by lightning

"like"

like father, like son; like mother, like daughter

not being able to do the limbo

Limburger cheese

people who hog the limelight

"You cannot escape history."—Abraham Lincoln

when the line you are in is invariably the slowest

long lines for public bathrooms

lint brushes that go the wrong way

lip synching

liposuction

people who don't listen

our litigious society

litterbugs

too little, too late

"Little Boxes" by Pete Seeger

Little League parents

when Beth March dies in *Little Women*

"Many a man has decided to stay alive, not because of the will to live, but because of the determination not to give assorted surviving bastards the satisfaction of his death."—Brandon Francis

living underneath really noisy people

living wills

venomous lizards

fear and loathing

lobbyists

lobotomies

dropping live lobsters into boiling water

local government

the Loch Ness Monster

lockjaw

coming home and finding all the locks changed

locking your keys in your car

swarms of locusts

logging

logorrhea

being a loner

a lonely hearts club

being lonely at the top

long commutes

trying to decide what long distance service to use

thinking you need to look different instead of being different

finding something in the *first* place you looked *after* searching through many other places

being looked up to

the loony bin

loopholes

loose and wanton women

looting

Los Angeles

losing

losing touch with reality

being lost in the boonies

lost causes

lost souls

lost trains of thought

greasy lotharios

not winning the lottery

people who think talking loudly to a person speaking a foreign language will make him/her understand English trying to figure out the words to "Louie, Louie"

things getting all loused up

love

"The Love Boat"

that love is blind (and deaf, mute, stupid . . .)

Love Canal

that the "Love Is" cartoon people never wear any clothes, except for when they go swimming and wear bathing suits

ex-lovers breezing through town

love triangles

all that lovey-dovey stuff

Willy Loman

being the low man on the totem pole

divided loyalties

the L.S.A.T.

Susan Lucci (Erica Kane on "All My Children") being nominated for the daytime Emmy for twelve years in a row, and never winning

Lucifer

losing your good luck charm

that Lucy, Ricky, Ethel, and Fred are all dead

getting somewhere and having your luggage
be somewhere better

lumps of coal in your stocking

lumpy liquid paper

the lunatic fringe

burning lungs

the *Lusitania*

lust

luxuries

swollen lymph nodes

lynch mobs

lying

the macabre

mace

Machiavelli

"Leave a message on my machine"

machine gun fire

machismo

macrame

going to bed mad

"See what you made me do?"

being made fun of

Madison Avenue

Madonna

the mafia

decorating magazines

telephone magazine subscription sellers

bad magicians

maggots

junk mail

trying to get off a mailing list

trying to make it through the night

trying to make every moment of your life matter

people who can't make up their minds

making the wrong move

malapropisms

malarkey

male chauvinist pigs

a malfunction of a fail-safe system

malicious mischief

malls

mall cops

tearing down beautiful old buildings with character to build mini-malls

The Maltese Falcon

manacles

middle management

confusing Manet and Monet

maniaphobia: the irrational fear of insanity

Barry Manilow

mankind

mannequins

man's inhumanity to man

Charles Manson

mantras

manure

leaving your map at home

fake maple syrup

playing the cello in a marching band

Imelda and Ferdinand Marcos

when your English teacher insists on narrow margins for your forty page essay on medieval literature

the Marines

marriage

when marriage counselors get divorced

marrying someone for their money, and then discovering they don't have any

re-marrying your ex-spouse, and having it not work out for the second time

being marooned

market research

marshes being drained

 martyrs

mascara streaks from crying

masochists

Jackie Mason

massage parlors

huddled masses

maternity clothes

math

when the springs pop through your mattress

being mauled by a grizzly bear

mausoleums

maxims

"Mayberry R.F.D."

May-December romances

"maybe"

mayflies

when your mayor is hauled off to jail

McCarthyism

McDonald's recruiting senior citizens to flip hamburgers

letters from Ed McMahon

not knowing where your next meal comes from

mealy worms

mean bosses

living beyond your means

measles

getting trapped in a meat locker

EVEN WORSE: swinging from a meathook

unethical and incompetent mechanics

meddling friends

medflies

media hype

medical boards

medical malpractice

Medicare

Medicare fraud

a dose of your own medicine

"Clawing and scratching your way to mediocrity"—Rick Dees

Medusa

melodrama

memos

memorabilia

when all you have are memories to sustain you

men

men who have feminine voices

men who "sprinkle" on the toilet seat

men who tell women that P.M.S. is all in their heads

menopause

menstrual cramps

mental blocks

mental fatigue

getting menthol in your eyes

mercenaries

merchandising

a strained quality of mercy

merging into heavy traffic

cleaning up someone else's mess

"We'll be right back after these messages."

metaphysics

slow metabolisms

a meteor making a big hole in your house

the metric system

Miami

"Miami Vice"

mouse heads in your canned vegetables

the fact that Mickey Mouse has a pet dog

microbursts

micropenis

reading microfiche

the story of the woman drying her cat in the microwave

midair collisions

"The really frightening thing about middle age is knowing you'll outgrow it."—Doris Day

the shrinking middle class

midlife crises

midterms

migrant workers

low mileage

mildew

"military intelligence"

military schools

realizing that there are not milk men to run away with anymore

milking something for all it's worth

millipedes

a millstone hanging around your neck

bad mimes

someone making mincemeat out of you

mind-boggling facts

mind control

mind games

mindless jobs

mini-series

minimum balances

minimum wage jobs

taking minutes at a meeting

hoping for a miracle

two-way mirrors

misanthropy

misappropriation of funds

miscasting

miscommunication

misconceptions

being fixated on misery

other people trying to get you to be
miserable about things you are not

people trying to make you happy when you
are miserable

"If misery loves company, misery has company enough."—Henry David Thoreau

all the things there are to be miserable about, but aren't in this book

whatever makes you miserable that makes other people happy

things that are misfiled

misfits

profiting from other people's misfortune

misgivings

being misinformed

misprizal

misreading tablespoon for teaspoon

Miss Congeniality

missing your baby's first step

missing your connecting flight

missing an easy shot

missing someone

knowing you're making a mistake even as you're making it

getting trapped under the mistletoe with someone you hate

being misquoted

Walter Mitty

mixed metaphors

moans and groans

mobile homes

being a mob informant

Moby Dick

water moccasins

the Middle Ages

modems

Molotov cocktails

absolute monarchy

"If you are sure you understand everything that is going on, you are hopelessly confused."—Walter Mondale

Monday

money

money burning a hole in your pocket

having your milk money stolen

people to whom money is no object

people who put a monetary value on everything

putting money into a car that's not worth fixing because you can't afford to buy a new one

a monkey on your back

monkey suits

mononucleosis

monopolistic mergers

getting stuck with the iron when playing Monopoly

monsters under your bed

Montezuma's revenge

no more Monty Python

mooching

mood swings

Moonies

realizing that the old "Mary Tyler Moore Show" doesn't hold up so well in reruns

sitting around moping

morality

the Moral Majority

low morale

morbidity

"more or less"

potluck dinners at the morgue

morning people

morning sickness

oxymorons

regular morons

confronting your own mortality

drive-through mortuaries

mosquitoes

motel hangers that are attached to the rod

hourly rate motels that don't change the
sheets

riding a motorcycle without a helmet

when your mother donates your favorite shirt
to charity because it was "old"

mothers

your mother-in-law

Mother Nature

motion sickness

Motley Crue

mousse

movie critics

movie theaters that don't honor passes

really lousy movies made from really good books

your best friend moving away

mowing the lawn

tracking mud in the house

looking through mug books

multiple personality disorder

mumbo jumbo

mummies

the mumps

the mundane

people who get away with murder

pulling a muscle

a lack of muscle tone

fickle muses

additional charges for special exhibits at museums

poison mushrooms

mushroom clouds

music boxes that play annoying songs over, and over, and over, and over. . .

mustard gas

mutation

mutiny

Muzak

the mysteries of life

myths

naked people

having a name you hate

trying to decide whether or not to change your name upon marriage

calling out the wrong name during a moment of passion

calling your children by the wrong names

napalm

Napoleon Bonaparte

"nap drool"

narcolepsy

narrow views

not knowing all of the words to the national anthem

the national debt

The National Enquirer

when you really wanted natural childbirth, but you end up needing drugs

the Navy

naysayers

Nazis

EVEN WORSE: neo-Nazis

nearsightedness

having no neck

needing something you can't ever get

not being needed

being needled

removing a stitch on your needlepoint and accidentally cutting the canvas

negative advertisements

double negatives

criminal negligence

gross negligence

nosy neighbors

neighbors with a pet rooster

trying to figure out what, other than picking up some tutti-fruity ice cream, Ozzie Nelson did

receiving a letter from your teacher, signed "your nemesis"

nepotism

nerve damage

nervous laughter

networking

"never mind"

New Coke

"new and improved"

New Kids on the Block

New Year's resolutions

New York City

trying to finish *The New York Times* crossword puzzle

the news

going over Niagara Falls in a barrel

"What's a nice girl like you doing in a place like this?"

a nickname you can't shake

night blindness

nightmares

Night of the Living Dead

night school

nihilists

shaving nicks

1–900 numbers

Nintendo

when it's really cold and your nipples pucker

nitrates in hot dogs

Richard M. Nixon

EVEN WORSE: Nixon's pardon

THE WORST: how well President Nixon and the people involved in Watergate are doing today

no

no way out

no-win situations

noise pollution

Oliver North

EVEN WORSE: the people above Oliver North who used him as a scapegoat

Northwest Airlines

cutting off your nose to spite your face

paying through the nose

wiping your sore nose with rough tissues

nosedives

nose hair

nostalgia

not knowing and not caring

being a notch on somebody's bed post

Cliff Notes

expecting nothing and getting less

having nothing left to lose

nothingness

"final notice prior to disconnection" notices

notoriety

nouvelle cuisine

novelties

noxious fumes

nuclear: deterrents, fallout, proliferation, terrorism, waste, weapons, winter being dressed at a nudist colony

"nuking" dinner

being forced to take a number in a store even when there are no other customers

defrocked nuns who smoke cigarettes, swill whiskey, and play poker late at night with adolescent boys

The Nuremberg Trials

that nursing home smell

people picking out all of the cashews from your box of mixed nuts

philosophies in a nutshell

nymphomania

oat bran

breaking an oath

the word "obey" in marriage vows

a lack of objectivity

being denied conscientious objector status

erroneous obituaries

obligations

the obliteration of all life on our planet

oblivion

obscene phone calls

obsessive/compulsive behavior

formidable obstacles

obstinance

an obvious plot

missing the obvious

the occult

mail addressed to "Occupant"

occupational hazards

ocean pollution

being tossed in the ocean with cement blocks tied to your feet

odds and ends

when the odds are three billion to one and you're the one

the odor of decay

an Oedipus complex

offal

being off the beaten track

off-color jokes

being deeply offended

two officials calling the same play differently

ogling

oikophobia: the abnormal fear of your house

oil leaks from your car

oil: sheiks, slicks, spills, of Olay

getting old

old flames

"For old time's sake"

your favorite song from high school being called an "oldie"

old wive's tales

Old Yeller

olive drab

the ombudsman

bad omens

people who tell you things are done when they are not

one-arm bandits

people who believe there is only one way

one night stands

"the one that got away"

one-upmanship

one way streets

chopping onions

the oompah loompahs

The Omen

onomatopoeia

"oops"

opaque windows in doctor's offices that are kept closed

open marriages

opening up

people opening car doors into traffic

being late for a one-act opera

opium dens

not answering your door when opportunity knocks

when opposites attract

oppressive regimes

opprobrious language

diametric oppositions

optical illusions

optimism and optimists

"The optimist thinks that this is the best of all possible worlds, and the pessimist knows it."
—J. Robert Oppenheimer

"or else"

the color orange

seeds in your orange juice

the ordinary

people who eat the middle out of all the Oreo cookies

organized religion

orgasmic impairment

orphanages

the Osmonds

ostentatiousness

being ostracized

Lee Harvey Oswald

other people

Ouija boards

ousted dictators who are allowed to live comfortably and undisturbed in other countries

being out of bounds

being out of control

"out of order"

going out of your mind

when your oven isn't baking at the right temperature

overbooking

overestimating yourself

overexposure

being overextended

overpopulation

being rejected for a job because you are overqualified

being told you are overreacting

overly simplistic philosophies

oversleeping

oversimplifications

overstaying your welcome

addiction to over-the-counter drugs

plotting to overthrow a government

people who owe you money

owing somebody more than you can ever repay

your oxygen tank running out when you're way below the surface

tainted oysters

the holes in the ozone layer

not packing the right stuff

paddy wagons

pagans

turning the pages in a book so fast they tear

being poorly paid

pain

"action painting"

paintings of people or animals with really big eyes

painting by numbers

a deathly pallor

pancake makeup

Pandora's box

panhandling

the panic button

getting panned

pantophobia: the abnormal fear of everything

plaid, polyester pants

a run in your pantyhose

women leaving their pantyhose hanging on
the shower curtain rod

the paparazzi

paper cuts

EVEN WORSE: paper cuts on your tongue

when parts of the Sunday paper are missing

pithy parables

skydiving without your parachute

parades

Paradise Lost

paranoia

parochialism

horrible intestinal parasites

being parched with thirst

your parents

parents who don't read to their children

not knowing who your parents are

your parents doing things with your children that you asked them not to

being told by your parents that the reason for something is because they are your parents

parenthetical explanations

forgetting to set the parking brake while on a hill

parking garages where you have to drive all the way up to get down

people who leave events before they're over in order to get out of the parking lot

no parking zones

not being able to find you car in the parking lot

no parking zones

not being able to find your car in the parking lot

a ludicrous parody

paroxysms

"party" as a verb

coming out parties

the party line

not knowing anyone at a party

pass interference

passing the buck

passport photos

not knowing the secret password

confronting your past

overcooked pasta

being slapped with a paternity suit

pathological liars

taxing your patience

being patronized

a fat paunch

paupers

Maury Povich

being pawed

a paycheck written in disappearing ink

paying the current cost of a movie ticket

paying through the nose

taking a paycut in order to keep your job

payola

"peace with honor"

"peachy keen"

screaming peacocks

peanut butter stuck to the roof of your mouth

comments from the peanut gallery

pecksnifferyism

peculiarities

pedants

those "pedestrian crossing" buttons at traffic lights

pedophiles

someone peeing in the top bunk while you are in the bottom

peeping Toms

peer pressure

pet peeves

peg legs

being penalized

penance

the demise of fountain pens

pencils with the erasers worn off

an out-of-whack penile implant

the Pentagon's black budget

that penguins have longer-lasting
monogamous relationships than humans do

"The People's Court"

people trying to talk you into things

"Have your people call my people"

people for whom things always work out

striving for perfection

perforated sheets that don't pull apart

performance art

getting your period

EVEN WORSE: *not* getting your period

THE WORST: getting your period on your
wedding day

perky people

when your perm flops

all those things that were "going on your
permanent record"

all the different permutations

the Persian Gulf

being stubbornly persistent

a perverse sense of humor

pesky varmints

pessimists

being pestered

dumb pet names

not being able to get your pet out of your burning house

when your pet rock hates you

the Peter Pan syndrome

phallic symbols

Philistines

phlegm

being charged for directory assistance

waiting for a phone call that never comes

answering machines for car phones

being charged *not* to publish your phone number

when the phone rings while you are soaking in the tub, and you run out to get it, dripping all over, and you get there just in time to hear a click

people *calling you* and then talking to other people while you're on the line

photocopied body parts

photo opportunities

phrenology

your sadistic P.E. instructor

physical therapy

forgetting to rinse out the picnic cooler and then opening it a year later

people who pick their teeth at the dinner table

crossing a picket line

crooked pictures

when your mother shows your baby pictures to other people

photos that don't turn out

your picture hanging in the post office

being pigeonholed

trying to make pie crust from scratch

pigeons

living like a pig

the pilot light burning out

pillows that have lost their fluff

the Pillsbury Doughboy

pimento loaf

pimps

squeezing pimples

pinching a whole lot more than an inch

someone pinching your cheeks

pinched nerves

Pink Floyd

pink plastic flamingos

a pink slip in your paycheck

the Ford Pinto

piranhas

pistol ranges

pit bulls

getting a pizza with the wrong toppings

when you work really hard on a paper for
school, and it turns out so good your teacher
accuses you of plagiarism

plaids made up of colors that don't go
together

dried up Play-doh

the best laid plans

plant closings

forgetting to water the plants

plastic surgery

Sylvia Plath

platitudinarians

playing the field

playing for more than you can afford to lose

when you're playing Scrabble and someone gets a word with a really high score that you are sure isn't a real word...so you look it up in the dictionary and it is

"Play Misty for Me"

trying to please everybody

exchanging pleasantries

The P.L.O.

plucking poultry

plumber's charges

trying to fix your own plumbing

plutocracy

plutonium

pneumonia

pneumonoultramicroscopicsilicovolcanoconiosis

poachers

poetic license

pogo sticks

pogroms

the point of no return

poison ivy

receiving poison pen letters

poison mushrooms

being poked in the eye with a sharp stick

playing poker with someone who cheats

the polar ice caps melting

inner city police precincts

police brutality

politics

political candidates

EVEN WORSE: political candidates who refuse to debate

political hacks and party bosses

politicians

being married to someone with opposing political views

exit polls

pollution

polo

polyester

"Pomp and Circumstance"

pond scum

sculpted poodles

pool hustlers

pooper-scoopers

being poor as a churchmouse

poor, naive old ladies who send televangelists all their money

being poor and living in an upperclass neighborhood

poor timing

pop with no fizz

popcorn hulls

popcorn kernels that don't pop

pop culture

pop psychology

when the popsicle breaks off the stick

pop quizzes

family portraits

people who are positive they are right

Emily Post

postcards that arrive after you do

"which you were here" postcards

Post-its

the United States Postal Service

running a large mailing through a postage
meter that was set with the wrong amount

continuously rising postal rates

posthumous recognition of your work

the pot calling the kettle black

pot pies

potatoes with eyes

potholes

your pound of flesh

"Poverty must have its satisfactions, else there would not be so many poor people."—Don Herold

the Powers That Be

power ties

being forced to practice what you preach

pragmatism

wedding party attendants who play pranks on your wedding night

high-tech prayer

praying mantises

bad precedents

not practicing what you preach

precociousness

predictions of the end of the world

preemptive air strikes

prejudice

premature ejaculation

premeditated crimes

premiums that don't make any sense with the product they are being given away with

being preoccupied while driving

prepared spontaneity

insufficient preparation

mistaking Preparation H for toothpaste

not being able to meet the prerequisites for a class you want to take

giving your children too many presents and not enough presence

"When I was a boy, I was told that anyone could become president. I'm beginning to believe it."—Clarence Darrow

the press

pretending you know what you are doing

trying to price your once-prized possessions for your garage sale

exorbitant prices

price-fixing

pride

swallowing your pride

prima donnas

primal scream therapy

Princeton University

when great books go out of print

people who believe everything they see
in print

having your priorities in the wrong order

"dial-a-prayer"

private investigators

prize fights

people who tell you worse problems in
response to hearing about yours

procrastination

large-fingered proctologists

professional conferences

prohibitive costs

prohibition

making promises you can't keep

being passed over for promotion

not being able to pronounce something

people who can't pronounce or spell your
name

people who don't proofread

false prophecies

having to write grant proposals

prostitution

protection money

Protestantism

people who insist that protesting a war is unsupportive of the troops

protesting too much

when the prototype works but the real thing doesn't

prudes

pseudo-intellectuals

a psychotherapist with a big mouth

psychic hotlines

taking a shower right after watching *Psycho*

psychedelia

psychological warfare

psychopathic killers

P.T.A. meetings

falling asleep in public

public speaking

public transportation

not being able to submit your work to a
publisher without a literary agent, and not
being able to get a literary agent without
being published

being pulled over

someone who pulls the wings off flies

having your wisdom teeth pulled

pumping iron

punching a time clock

people who pun and say "no pun intended"

punctuation

punishment

punks

punting

dilated pupils

purgatory

Puritanism

not having a purple crayon

purple prose

losing your purse

pus

people who push in line

pushing up daisies

pushing yourself too hard

people who don't put things back where they belong

pyramid schemes

discovering your fire chief is a pyromaniac

pushing a Q-tip in too far

"quality time"

quaaludes

"quantities may be limited"

armchair quarterbacks

close quarters

Quasimodo

J. Danforth Quayle

hopeless quests

things that are none of your business but you want to know anyway

people who ask you questions that they know are none of their business

unanswerable questions

questioning authority

quitting

quota systems

racial slurs

racing forms

the rack

broken tennis racquet strings

planes disappearing from radar

radiccio

the distortion of a radio with low batteries

radioactive wastes

radon

when someone you knew thirty-five years ago calls you out of the blue, yells at you, calls you names, and slams the phone in your ear

ragweed

having your softball game rained out

chasing rainbows

destroying the rainforests

when it's raining cats and dogs

freezing rain

"Rainy Days and Mondays" by the Carpenters

stepping on a rake

Rambo

ransom notes

rappers

raping and pillaging

being rapped on the knuckles with a ruler

rash statements

rat poison

the rat race

rationing

Dan Rather

the ravages of time

reaching into the bottom of an ice-filled barrel for a can of pop

reaching into a public washroom's paper towel disposal and being pricked by a used hypodermic needle

that for every action there is a reaction

not getting the reaction you expected

being forced to read long, bad, boring books

not being ready

reading between the lines

"Everywhere we go Nancy makes the world a little better."—Ronald Reagan

"One way to make sure crime doesn't pay would be to let the government run it."—Ronald Reagan

"I'm not smart enough to lie."—Ronald Reagan

real estate agents

reality

the moment you realize your child may never live at home again

reasoning with a four year old

campus rebels

rebel factions

being on the rebound

recanted testimony

receiving something C.O.D. that you didn't order

bad reception due to solar activity

unpleasant receptionists

recession

recliners that are too close to the wall and therefore don't recline

recognizing someone, but being unable to remember from where

not recognizing yourself when you look in the mirror

having to reconsider

asking for paper bags at the store and having them put everything in plastic bags before putting it into the paper bags

trying to recycle in a community that doesn't

red alerts

red hot pokers

when your C.P.A. sends out for more red ink

Vanessa Redgrave

red tape

that Robert Redford is married

redundancies, over and over again

the chopping down of California redwoods

reenacting childhood trauma

news stories that use unlabeled reenactments

referees

loud noises in the reference room

poor reflexes

not being able to refold your road map

knowing you can't reform the world

political reform

being a refugee

regal horned lizards

regulations

reigns of terror

rejection letters

"I can relate"

love/hate relationships

a relationship in which the only appeal is the danger

a person with whom you are pursuing a relationship who is moving too fast

signing release forms

religious fundamentalism

remakes

being unable to remember your name

the more you try to think of something you are trying to remember the harder it becomes

when you're happily singing a song and then get to the part where you can't remember the words

being unable to remember the word for something

remorse

the inability to turn live people off with a TV remote control

Renaissance tragedy

not getting the rental car you ordered

repair people who can't keep their pants up

when the cost of repair is worth more than the item itself

trying to get repair help on a holiday weekend

"One way to get high blood pressure is to go mountain climbing over molehills."—Earl Wilson

reporters having to go to jail in order to protect their sources

EVEN WORSE: reporters revealing their sources

being reprimanded

the Republicans

your reputation preceding you

people who don't pull over for rescue vehicles with their sirens on

artificial respiration

exhausting your resources

being a responsible person

people who don't take responsibility for themselves

restaurants that don't take reservations

when you discover a really wonderful restaurant, with great food, terrific service, and reasonable prices, and then lots of other people discover it, it gets crowded and expensive, the waitstaff turns snotty, and the food gets bad

restless natives

"No Rest Areas for the Next Eighty-seven Miles"

résumés

losing your retainer

retardation

people who don't know what to do with themselves after they retire

hasty retreats

return cards that don't fit into return envelopes

needing to return something, but not having the receipt

reunions of old TV shows

"Reveille"

revenge

reversals of fortune

reverse discrimination

reading a review of your work

revisions

revolving doors

"I'll still respect you in the morning"

rheumatism

people who rhyme all the time

the rhythm method

fatty ribs

rice thrown at weddings that harm little birds

get-rich-quick schemes

the rich getting richer and the poor getting poorer

climbing on a rickety chair

riddles

riding out a storm

being taken for a ride

rigamarole

rigor mortis

people who are always right

rites of passage

mood rings

when your ring is on too tight and you can't get it off

married folks who don't wear wedding rings

ringing in your ears

ringworm

"Ripley's Believe It or Not"

"rise and shine"

dried out riverbeds

Joan Rivers

roach motels

road kill

being the guest of honor at a roast

bank robbers

robbing Peter to pay Paul

Oral Roberts

Mrs. Robinson

falling rocks

rocks in your head

"Rock-a-bye Baby"

rocking the boat

"Rocky" movies

"Last year we said, 'things can't go on like this,' and they didn't . . . they got worse."—Will Rogers

thinking about what would happen to the world if all Mr. Rogers's sweaters unraveled

role playing

role reversal

being stuck upside down on a broken roller coaster

the fall of the Roman Empire

romance

realizing that Romeo and Juliet are actually nitwits

hitting the roof

leaky roofs

rookies replacing veterans

not having your own room

roommates

Andy Rooney

root canals

rose chafer beetles

ruthlessness

Pete Rose

"Rosebud"

a late frost that kills all your rose bushes

Rosencrantz and Guildenstern

a round-the-clock watch

a change in your routine

people who don't R.S.V.P.

being rubbed the wrong way

burning rubber

eing shot with a rubber band

when you try to make a rubber band fit around something, and it *almost* does, and then it snaps

feather boas

being whipped with a rubber hose

Betty Rubble's annoying voice

crossing the Rubicon

Rubik's Cube

rebuttals

rudeness

when all the other reindeer wouldn't let poor Rudolph play in any reindeer games

ruffled feathers

having the rug pulled out from under you

the road to ruin

ruing the day you were born

rules

breaking the rules

getting the run-around

run-on sentences

children running into the street

if you stop running long enough to feel the heaviness in your legs, and then try to start again

running against the wind

running into someone you used to be very close to but have fallen out of touch with, and not having a thing to say

running for your life

runts

rush hour traffic

rushing a fraternity or sorority

Russian roulette

cattle rustlers

being in a rut

ruthlessness

discovering you were using the wrong calendar to determine the dates for birth control by the rhythm method

people who don't know the difference between plural and possessive S ("Yes! We now serve hamburger's!")

saccharine-coated people

Sacco and Vanzetti

being sacked

wandering around in sackcloth and ashes

sacrificial sheep

sadists

sadness

"Nothing is said that has not been said before."—Terence

a hole in your sail

people touching the food and serving bowls with their fingers at a salad bar

ordering your salad dressing on the side and not getting it that way

the Salem witch trials

cosmetics salespeople who wear too much make-up

persistent salespeople

sales tax

mistaking salt for sugar

people who salt their food without tasting it first

doing the same thing every day

the San Diego Chicken

being denied sanctuary

sand storms

a sanitation workers' strike

discovering there is no Santa Claus

EVEN WORSE: when your child discovers
there is no Santa Claus

THE WORST: department store Santas
molesting their little patrons

sarcasm

when you are really mean to people and they
are too stupid to know it

satire

satyriasis

falling satellites

reaching your saturation point

Saturday night specials

the Saudi government

things you have clearly painstakingly saved,
but are unable to remember why

the S & L crisis

not knowing what to say

what people say behind your back

anyone who says, "I don't smoke, the cigarette does"

people who say "newclur" instead of "nuclear"

thinking of the right thing to say too late to say it

people who say, "There's good news, and there's bad news"

the good news

the bad news

saying yes when you want to say no, and saying no when you want to say yes

scabs

scaffolds

when the scale doesn't go up as high as you do

ticket scalpers

scamming

scandal

scanning the radio in a vain attempt to find a decent song

scapegoats

scarification

being scared out of your wits

scary-looking hooded robes

scathing reviews

scatology

scattered showers

Phyllis Schlafly

school boards

the school of hard knocks

school lunch menus

a lack of confidence in our public schools

school plays

school prayer

Arnold Schwarzenegger

science fairs

schisms

dull scissors

being scooped

scorpions

playing Scrabble and having a Q but no U

scratches on your new car

blood-curdling screams

holes in the screens

scrooges

scrounging around

scrubbing grout with a toothbrush

scuffs on your new hardwood floor

the scum of the earth

getting seasick

baby seals getting
clubbed over the head

seances

search and destroy missions

the search for greatness

automatic seat belts

being seated next to someone you can't stand
at a formal affair

playing second fiddle

secondary infections

secretaries who can't spell

bad sectors

passing through a security checkpoint without being checked

seduction

when someone can see through you

seeing the world through rose-colored glasses

seeking and never finding

segregation

having to register for Selective Service in order to receive educational financial aid

self-actualization

self-destruction

self-help books

self-reliance

selling out

seminars

sensationalized headlines

not having the sense to come out of the rain

bombardment of your senses

sensitivity training

senseless violence

sentence fragments

sugary sentimentality

when church and state aren't separated

septic tanks

sequels

serial murder

not being taken seriously

taking yourself too seriously

a serpent's tooth

poor service

nutritional labelling information based on ridiculous serving sizes

settling for less

anyone who doesn't like Dr. Seuss

the seven year itch

severing digits

sewers backing up into your house

sex

lack of sex

having sex in a bed of poison oak

colleges that cover up sex crimes involving their students

sex change operations

sex with your dead mother

"sex, drugs, rock and roll"

sexual harassment

sex kittens

sex, lies, and videotape

everything you have always wanted to know
about sex, but were afraid to ask...really

sexploitation

oral sex while driving

walking in on your parents having sex

sex slaves

sexually transmitted diseases

needing a blood test before sex

sex without love

punitive withholding of sex

sexism

shadows

the shadow of death

walking in someone's shadow

the Shah of Iran

people who insist Shakespeare was really somebody else

EVEN WORSE: people who think Shakespeare was Christopher Marlowe

THE WORST: that we are not allowed to shoot them

sharing

teeny little shards of glass in your foot that you can feel but can't get out

sharks

Al Sharpton

being shaved before surgery

shell shock

sheepdip

fitted sheets that won't stay on

working incredibly hard on a project that gets shelved

children pulling things off the shelves at the grocery store

shenanigans

shielding children from the truth

The Shining

bruised shins

a ship of fools

ships passing in the night

shipwrecks

"plus shipping and handling"

shivers up your spine

shock treatment

shoddy work

gum on the bottom of your shoe

walking in the rain with a hole in your shoe

drinking shoe polish

a rock in your shoe

smelly gym shoes

walking out of the bathroom with toilet paper
stuck to the bottom of your shoe

a broken shoelace

Christmas shopping

when the wheels of your shopping cart go in
different directions

shopping for your first car

shopping for your first bra

213

shopping sprees you can't afford

people who think shopping is a sport

sand in your shorts

shortsightedness

food shortages

short-sheeted beds

shots

shotgun weddings

the stack of newspapers and magazines you are saving because you "really should" read them

shoveling snow

showdowns

cold showers

showoffs

shower curtains gone bad

shrapnel embedded in your body

Shriners

shriveled-up fingers

shriveling up and dying

shrouds

walking into a room and having everybody instantly become silent

sibling rivalry

getting sick

EVEN WORSE: getting sick when it's hot

THE WORST: getting sick and having to clean it up

getting sick the day you are supposed to leave on vacation

needing surgery in a strange, foreign country

sick puppies

never getting the opportunity to tell your side of the story

side effects

signing on the dotted line

people who don't signal before changing lanes

signs on people's front doors announcing who they are

the silent treatment

leaking silicone breast implants

dinner guests making off with the silver

215

silverfish

the moment that you realize you did it even though Simon didn't say

"All simple statements are wrong."—Frank Knight

the wages of sin

singalongs

lounge singers

singles bars

"swinging singles"

sinister laughter

sinking money into a losing venture

being on a sinking ship

Siskel and Ebert (sometimes)

the myth of Sisyphus

sisters

a sitting duck

situational ethics

when "60 Minutes" comes looking for you

working with a skeleton crew

skeletons in your closet

skid row

your skin crawling

jewelry that turns your skin green

skinheads

skin flicks

the smell of a skunk that's been run over

when the sky is dark and threatening

crashing through the skylight

when Luke Skywalker discovers Darth Vader
is his father

slander

slaphappiness

being slapped

slash and burn farming

slasher movies

slaving over a hot stove

sledgehammers

sleeping with your boss

feeling something moving in the bottom of
your sleeping bag

sleeping with someone who snores

sleepwalking

sleet

sleazy men wearing low-cut polyester shirts with the buttons undone and gold chains

sleight of hand

slim pickings

slime molds

slinging hash

the slings and arrows of outrageous fortune

when your slinky gets stretched too far

letting something slip

when your slip is showing

letting something slip through your fingers

slobs

slot machines

driving behind slow people

slugs

slum lords

a batting slump

slush

small children who ask annoying questions repeatedly

making small talk
small town newspapers
smart alecks
smear campaigns
smiley faces
people who smirk
smog alerts
smoke screens
people who smoke
the smoking gun
smooth operators
smudges on important papers
the Smurfs
snafus
snaps that don't snap anymore
snarling dogs
sneezing in your hand
snide comments
snipers
frozen snot

yellow snow

snow globes

the city snow plow plowing a pile directly into your driveway

John Sununu

"so many books, so little time"

talking about the things that happen on your soap opera as though they're real

dropping the soap in the shower

soap scum

sobering thoughts

social diseases

the society page

knee socks that don't stay up

mismatched socks

the trial of Socrates

what you find in the crevices of your sofa

software glitches

S.O.L.

solar flares

losing at solitaire

solicitation

when a singer screws up one of your favorite songs

having a song racing through your head and not being able to get it out

songs with lyrics you can't understand

when what you want to come later comes sooner, and what you want to come sooner comes later

sophistry

a sordid past

sore losers

when your throat is so sore it hurts to swallow

"When sorrows come, they come not single spies, but in battalions."—William Shakespeare

bombing sorties

S.O.S.

fallen souffles

soul-searching

being a sensitive soul

South Africa

sowing your wild oats

the Space Shuttle

things that just take up space

people invading your space

spaghetti westerns

Spam

the Spanish-American war

sparks coming out of your light socket

lovers' spats

being spat upon

believing someone when they tell you you are special

being at risk as a spectator at an athletic event

speech impediments

speed traps

when the freezer breaks down at the sperm bank

a low sperm count

spewing soda through your nose

spiders

when your daughter brings home a boy
named Spike

spilling red wine on your antique white lace
tablecloth

spilling your guts

spin control

spinach stuck in your front teeth

evil spirits

gobs of spit on the sidewalk

spitballs

spittlebugs

being splattered with hot grease

splinters under your fingernails

split infinitives

spontaneity

sports records with asterisks

unsportsmanlike behavior

spouses

spouses who have an affair and then tell to
ease *their* conscience

finding out your spouse is sleeping with your
best friend

EVEN WORSE: finding out your spouse is sleeping with your sibling

THE WORST: discovering your spouse/significant other has left you for a member of the same sex

kids on spring break

spring fever

springing a leak in your boat

spies

squalling babies

square dancing

going back to square one

finding square roots

squid

being stabbed in the back

staff meetings

stage fright

blood stains

high stakes

stakeouts

being stalked

Sylvester Stallone

licking stamps

when the post office raises the amount to mail a first-class letter, and you have to buy supplements in order to use the stamps you already have

lowering the standards of what our children need to learn in order to get through school

standing out in a crowd

staples stuck in the stapler

"Star Search"

being stared at

having to start life all over again

starting from the ground up

starving children living in your own town

stasiophobia: the irrational fear of standing up

state government

the State of the Union address

static cling

statistics

status symbols

the status quo

stepping on a rusty nail

stereotypes

steroids

Martha Stewart

the short end of the stick

the sticker price

sticking your neck out

an old stick in the mud

a sticky wicket

sticky movie theater floors

stick-ups

maintaining a stiff upper lip

making a big stink

stinkbombs

the stockade

not taking a stock tip that would have ended up making you a *lot* of money

stock market crashes

stoics

unknowingly receiving stolen goods

stomach pumps

when your stomach makes loud, embarrassing noises

getting stoned

being stood up

only knowing part of the story

the story of your life

story problems

a strange car parked in front of your house

strange people putting their hands in your mouth

being on a plane, bus, or train with strangers who want to talk to you

strangulation

SDI

the straw that breaks the camel's back

strays

stress

streets with no street signs

stretch marks

strip searches

strobe lights

men who think they are real studs

paying back your student loans

student nurses

studying for finals

stuffed animals that aren't soft

being stumped

styrofoam

the subjugation of women

subliminal advertising

subpoenas

the government subsidizing tobacco farmers

substandard English

substandard housing

restaurants that don't allow substitutions

suburbia and suburbanites

never experiencing success

sucker punches

people who come out of the woodwork to lay their claims on your success

sudden death

needing permission from the government to sue the government

when sugar is listed as the first ingredient in your cereal

the power of suggestion

calling a suicide hotline and being put on hold

sullen teenagers

sullying your good name

summer

doing several somersaults in a row and then standing up

sunburn

Sunset Strip

whatever is on the other channels during the Super Bowl

all the people who can't see the resemblance between Clark Kent and Superman

superstitions you don't *actually* believe, but can't help just wondering about

supervillains

supply-side economics

support groups

suppositories

the Supreme Court

surgeons leaving sponges in

the government's surplus cheese

the element of surprise

accidentally blowing a surprise party

surrealism

being under surveillance

sushi

being suspected of something you didn't do

EVEN WORSE: being suspected of something you did do

Jimmy Swaggart

swamp gas

swan songs

swastikas

swearing

waking up in a cold sweat

sweatshops

swimmer's ear

people who sit right next to a swimming pool
and complain about getting splashed

the *Sports Illustrated* swimsuit issue

flimsy swingsets

switchblades

synonyms

someone setting a tab at every single space
on your typewriter

a table with one shorter leg than the others

tabloids

biting into a taco and having the contents fall
out the other side

the tags on pillows and mattresses that say
"do not remove under penalty of law"

dragging your tail

tailgaters

that you can't take it with you

being taken for granted

when everything takes longer than you
thought it would

people who talk in a foreign language you
don't speak when you are in the room

being talked about in the third person when you're in the room

people who like to hear themselves talk

not being able to remember which lie you told which person

talking Coke machines

people who talk during a movie

when one person talks but the whole class has to stay after school

tangled mobiles

not enough tape on the roll

tapeworms

eating tapioca pudding and feeling like little eyeballs are rolling around in your mouth

Jerry Tarkanian

tarpits

tarot cards

tattoos

taxes

tax breaks for the wealthy

cheating on your taxes

EVEN WORSE: when the I.R.S. comes for you

taxi drivers who don't know where they are
going

the taxing of student grants

boring teachers

the Teamsters

a lack of team spirit

Teenage Mutant Ninja Turtles

teenagers

when your teenage children are embarrassed
to be seen with you

telethons

televangelists

"Do you want to talk about it?"

temper tantrums

taking your temperature

when your temporary replacement is better
than you

being led into temptation

tension so thick you can cut it with a knife

tentacles

not getting tenure

terrorism

poison oak on your testicles

the Tet Offensive

The Texas Chainsaw Massacre

writing thank-you notes

thankless tasks

no one dressing for the theatre anymore

forgetting your theater tickets

rectal thermometers

theorems

thieves

thingamajigs

thing that go bump in the night

being told what someone thinks you want to hear

not having enough time to think about things

think tanks

"any enterprise that requires new clothes"—
Henry David Thoreau

a thorn in your side

one of *those* days

Three Mile Island
the Three Stooges
thrill seekers
throwing in the towel
being thrown into a pool with your clothes on
thumbscrews
thunderstorms
a nervous tic
getting a ticket for driving too slow
tickling
being tied up
loud ties
getting your tie caught in your fly
"As Time Goes By"
a walking time bomb
marking time
time-share apartments
Times Square
tips
when you are too tired for sex

the *Titanic*

today is the first day of the rest of your life

Sweeney Todd

toe cheese

having your toes chopped off with a machete

"We'll get back to you"

tofu ice cream

a toga party in your house

staying together for the sake of the children

overflowing toilets

discovering you are out of toilet paper—
too late

toilet paper with wood chunks in it

token minorities

having no money as you approach a tollbooth

waking up with a fuzzy tongue

having your tonsils removed as an adult

people who squeeze toothpaste from the
middle of the tube

torch songs

being torn between two lovers

torn rotator cuffs

tornados

torpedos

"Why torture yourself when life will do it for you?"—Laura Walker

torture chambers

totalitarianism

having no one to teeter your totter

those touchie-feelie types

touching cold metal with your tongue

touched-up photos

bad toupees

tourist attractions

broken toys

when someone beats you to the toy in the cereal box

the trade-in value of your car

trading arms for hostages

ancient traditions

traffic court

trains without cabooses

railroad crossing gates that go down when there's no train

falling asleep on a train and missing your stop

broken traffic signals

tragic heroes

fixed trials

transcendental meditation

putting in for a transfer and being denied

blood transfusions

hair transplants

the confusion felt by a transvestite in a unisex salon

falling through a trapdoor while exploring an abandoned old mansion

being trapped inside a burning building

when your cat gets stuck in a tree

trying to figure out which came first, the chicken or the egg

long discussions that eventually erupt into late-night arguments about unanswerable philosophical questions

Trekkies

trench warfare

fashion trends

trial and error

that kids can't trick or treat on Halloween anymore

Trojan horses

troubled waters

getting trounced

Donald Trump

trusting souls

"You can trust me"

"All truths are half-truths."—Alfred North Whitehead

the moment of truth

trying to figure out the difference between partly sunny and partly cloudy

trying to have it all

trying to please everybody

tsetse flies

college tuition

when the light at the end of the tunnel is a speeding train coming right at you

Tupperware

Ted Turner and Jane Fonda

the twelfth leftover turkey meal you've eaten after Thanksgiving

any of the milestone birthdays (i.e. twenty-one, thirty, forty, fifty, etc.)

turning yourself inside out

jumping turnstiles

when tweezers lose their spring

trying to remember the words to the "Twelve Days of Christmas"

people who insist that twelve step programs are the answer to *everything*

"If you pick up a starving dog and make him prosperous, he will not bite you. This is the principle difference between a dog and a man."—Mark Twain

having a twenty-four hour bug for forty-eight hours

no more "Twilight Zone"

identical twins who switch places

when your twin forgets your birthday

typing something long and boring

taking two steps forward and one step back

typhoons

tpyos

Mike Tyson

UFO sightings

feeling like an ugly duckling

ulcers

ulterior motives

ultra suede

umpires

an unbalanced load

"There is only one thing about which I am certain, and this is that there is very little about which one can be certain."—William Somerset Maugham

Uncle Tom's Cabin

saying things that are uncalled for

seats in public places that are purposefully made uncomfortable

the undead

the underclass

receiving a sample of "Depends" undergarments

241

going underground

underlings

edible underwear

that there is "overwhelmed" and "underwhelmed" but no "whelmed"

unemployment

EVEN WORSE: the taxing of unemployment benefits

unexplainable phenomena

unfinished business

unjust laws

that which is uninspired

trade unions

unmentionables

EVEN WORSE: mentioning them

being unqualified

EVEN WORSE: being overqualified

unregistered firearms

unseasonably cold weather

unwanted advice

unwed mothers

being up to no good

not knowing which way is up

dressing completely in Saran Wrap with strategically placed red bows, extra-dry martini in hand, expecting your spouse... and instead opening the door to the UPS delivery person

a right-side-up upside-down cake

the uptight

uranium

urban decay

urinalysis

the United States playing cop to the world

used car salespeople

the amazing storage your brain has for useless information

utopias

Uzi assault weapons

dream vacations gone bad

the first day back from vacation

Valentine's Day

valet parking attendants who ding your car

the valley of the shadow of death

having friends with radically different value systems

vandalism

fake vanilla

varicose veins

that yucky scum that collects at the bottom of a vase of flowers

a botched vasectomy

people who can't work VCRs

how they get veal

mushy vegetables

vegeburgers

wanting to be a vegetarian, but liking meat

velcro

Velveeta "cheese"

paintings on velvet

vendettas

losing your money in a vending machine

vengeance

inadequate ventilation

ventriloquists

vermin

the vernacular

verisimilitude

vertigo

paralyzed veterans

being vetoed

vicious circles

being victimized

victims who don't press charges

video games

the Viet Cong

the Village People

vinyl

violations of your civil liberties

your own violent tendencies

vipers

sacrificial virgins

viruses

virtual reality

poor night vision

vitamin deficiency

vivisection

a limited vocabulary

the voices in your head arguing loudly

"void where prohibited"

high voltage fences

being volunteered for something

praying to the porcelain god

voodoo

voting against someone instead of for someone

a spare tire around your waist

waiters who pretend they are your friends

waiting in line

people who say "Just wait until next year"

EVEN WORSE: next year

waiving your rights

waking up in the morning

Kurt Waldheim

a walk on the wild side

people who walk backwards in dark houses in horror movies

walking under a ladder

when the walls have ears

Wall Street

the Wandering Jew

wanderlust

war

war euphoria

children thinking war pictures on TV are just a show

"You can't say that civilization don't advance. . . . For in every war they kill you in a new way."—Will Rogers

warm fuzzies

being truly warped

warped door jams

a warrant for your arrest

washing the windows

being stung by a wasp

waste

watching someone die

designer water

a leak in your waterbed

running out of hot water while your hair is full of shampoo

walking in stocking feet on a freshly waxed floor

a weak bladder

the weather

TV weatherpeople

how the weather affects your moods

webworms

weddings

losing your wedding band

your ex-lover's wedding

someone objecting at your wedding

planning a wedding

having your future spouse faint during your wedding vows

weeding

working twenty-five hours a day, eight days a week

weightlifting

Weight Watchers

the welcome wagon

Lawrence Welk

waking up just before the fulfillment of a wet dream

sitting in wet paint

beached whales

"Wheel of Fortune"

whips

people who can whip up great meals from nothing

white collar crime

white supremacists

Vanna White

whodunits

"To whom it may concern"

whoopee cushions

"I said so, that's why"

"Why did the chicken cross the road?"

wickedness

the Wicked Witch of the West

widgets

weirdos

a nagging wife

the call of the wild

wildfires

wild goose chases

people fighting over wills

living wills

the windchill factor

leaving your car windows open and having it rain

windows that are painted shut

tilting at windmills

wine tastings

Oprah Winfrey

Winnebagos

winning a prize only to be told that the rules disqualify you

winter

wiretapping

that wishing doesn't make it so

wishes that come true

wishing you were never born

wishing someone dead

EVEN WORSE: having them die

wisps of hair combed to cover a bald spot

the witching hour

withdrawal

withered crops

tales of woe

being woken up by someone who says, "Did I wake you?"

someone scrubbing clean your perfectly seasoned wok

women

a woman scorned

wondering

wood shop

itchy wool

words with "e"s added to them in order to make them look classier, like "Ye Olde Donut Shoppe"

being at a loss for words

work

believing in whatever works

taking work home with you

convicts not returning from work release

"You'll never work in this town again"

wanting to save the world

"This world is a comedy to those that think, a tragedy to those that feel."—Horace Walpole

worldwide ecological disaster

biting into an apple and finding half of a worm

worrying

EVEN WORSE: worrying that you worry too much

salt in your wounds

car wrecks

wrecking balls

mud wrestling

lights at Wrigley Field

writing blank checks

writing what you think the reader wants to
read, instead of what you want to write

writer's block

that nobody writes letters anymore

the writing on the wall

that which is neither right nor wrong

wrong numbers

being in the wrong place at the wrong time

Deng Xiaopeng

X-rays

yak meat

"ya know?"

the New York Yankees

yeast infections

yes

yes men

walking through the streets of yesteryear

ex-yippies who have become yuppies

yodeling

yoga

"yo mama"

the days of yore

people who are younger than you

people who are older than you

'You break it, you buy it"

"You know what I mean."

zealots

zen hipsters

a great big zero

zero coupon bonds

the zero hour

zigging when you should be zagging

zippers with missing teeth

getting your zipper caught on an important body part

zits

zoo animals

realizing this isn't even a small fraction of all the things there are to be miserable about in the world

ABOUT THE AUTHOR

Susan Klingman doesn't want to talk about it.